W9-AOU-123

DISCARD

CULTURES OF THE WORLD
Fiji

Roseline NgCheong-Lum

Marshall Cavendish
Benchmark
New York

PICTURE CREDITS
Cover: © Jon Arnold Images/Danita Delimont
Alamy: 16 • alt.type/Reuters: 27, 35, 36, 45, 79, 80, 90, 96, 97 • Art Director's and Trip: 20, 57, 95, 99, 107 • Audrius Tomonis:
135 • Corbis: 14, 52, 62, 77, 81 • Dave G. Houser: 23, 71, 103, 123 • Getty Images: 19, 21, 22, 28, 29, 30, 31, 33, 39, 61, 69,
73, 74, 76, 88, 98, 110, 112, 114, 125 • Haga Library, Japan: 105 • HBL Network Photo Agency: 102 • Hutchison Library:
47, 78, 91, 106, 119 • Lonely Planet Images: 11, 42, 70, 83, 109, 117, 118, 120, 124, 126, 127, 128 • Photolibrary: 1, 3, 5, 6,
7, 8, 9, 10, 12, 13, 17, 18, 24, 34, 38, 40, 41, 43, 44, 46, 49, 50, 51, 53, 54, 55, 56, 58, 60, 63, 64, 65, 66, 68, 72, 75, 82, 84,
85, 86, 87, 89, 92, 93, 104, 108, 111, 113, 116, 121, 129 • Tan Chung Lee: 100, 115, 122 • Topfoto: 48 • Trip Photographic
Agency: 122

PRECEDING PAGE
Gorgeous Fijian mountains framed by the intensely blue South Pacific Ocean waters in Fiji.

Publisher (U.S.): Michelle Bisson
Editors: Deborah Grahame, Mindy Pang
Copyreader: Daphne Hougham
Designers: Nancy Sabato, Lynn Chin
Cover picture researcher: Connie Gardner
Picture researcher: Thomas Khoo

Marshall Cavendish Benchmark
99 White Plains Road
Tarrytown, NY 10591
Website: www.marshallcavendish.us

© Times Media Private Limited 2000
© Marshall Cavendish International (Asia) Private Limited 2011
® "Cultures of the World" is a registered trademark of Times Publishing Limited.

Originated and designed by Times Media Private Limited
An imprint of Marshall Cavendish International (Asia) Private Limited
A member of Times Publishing Limited

Marshall Cavendish is a trademark of Times Publishing Limited.

All Internet sites were correct and accurate at the time of printing. All monetary figures in this publication are in U.S.
dollars unless otherwise stated.

Library of Congress Cataloging-in-Publication Data
NgCheong-Lum, Roseline, 1962-
  Fiji / Roseline Ng Cheong-Lum. — 2nd ed.
    p. cm. — (Cultures of the world)
  Includes bibliographical references and index.
  Summary: "Provides comprehensive information on the geography, history,
    wildlife, governmental structure, economy, cultural diversity, peoples,
    religion, and culture of Fiji"—Provided by publisher.
  ISBN 978-1-60870-022-6
  1. Fiji—Juvenile literature. I. Title.
  DU600.N45 2010
  996.11—dc22   2010000731

Printed in China
7 6 5 4 3 2 1

CONTENTS

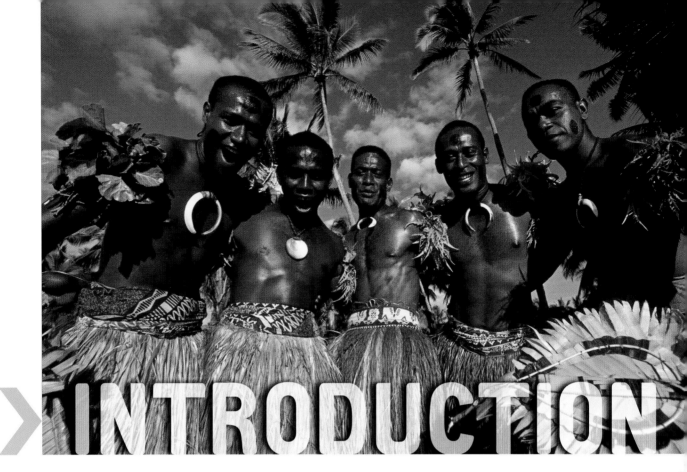

INTRODUCTION

CALLED THE GATEWAY TO THE SOUTH PACIFIC, FIJI IS A crossroad of cultures. This archipelago consists of some 330 volcanic islands and low-lying atolls. White sandy beaches, shifting sand dunes, colorful coils of reefs teeming with marine life, and impenetrable rain forests all form part of Fiji's landscape. Once feared for their reputation as fierce cannibals, Fiji Islanders today are among the most friendly people on Earth. The population consists of Fijians, Indians, Polynesians, Chinese, and Europeans, who live side by side as separate groups. While calling Fiji their home, the migrant communities have each retained their ancestral religions, customs, and cultures. In the course of a tumultuous history, the nonindigenous Fiji Islanders have suffered grave injustices. Moreover, the whole population has endured long-standing oppression as a result of the struggles between various factions in charge of the country. Hope rises that Fiji Islanders may soon enjoy the freedoms they are entitled to as citizens of a sovereign nation.

GEOGRAPHY

An aerial view of uninhabited Kuata Island, that is part of the Yasawa Group. There are so many islands in Fiji that it is often possible to have a whole stretch of sand and sea to oneself.

CHAPTER 1

SPRAWLING ACROSS AN AREA OF about 501,800 square miles (1,300,000 square kilometers) in the fabled South Seas, the Fijian archipelago is made up of 332 islands, of which about one-third are inhabited. Lying just north of the Tropic of Capricorn, the country is slightly larger than California and Nevada put together. Less than 1.5 percent of the area is land (7,056 square miles or 18,274 square km); the rest is open sea.

Fiji's Qamea Island has many rugged hills and beautiful beaches and lagoons.

The 180° meridian, the International Date Line that divides the world into today (on the west side) and yesterday (on the east side), passes through the islands. The date line, however, has been bent east so that the country is not split into two days. Fiji is the dividing point between the old divisions of Melanesia and Polynesia. To the east are the low coral atolls and volcanic islands of Polynesia. Moving west, the mountainous volcanic and continental islands of Melanesia arise.

The nearest large city is Auckland, New Zealand, which is located about 1,300 miles (2,092 km) to the south. Honolulu is only 5 hours away by air, while Los Angeles is a 10-hour flight.

THE FIJIAN ARCHIPELAGO

Fiji is composed of two large islands, Viti Levu and Vanua Levu, ringed by groups of smaller islands. The whole archipelago surrounds the Koro Sea.

Dusk settling serenely over Suva, the capital of Fiji.

The largest island is Viti Levu. Meaning "Big Fiji," it is the third-largest of all the islands in the Pacific and is the hub of the Fijian archipelago. Also the most developed island in the archipelago, Viti Levu is home to 70 percent of the Fijian population. One peculiarity of this island is the astonishing contrast between the east and west halves. While the eastern side is lushly wet and green, the western part is dry and sun-baked. It is the western coast that most tourists visit and where large areas of sugarcane plantations are located.

The Sigatoka River Valley in Viti Levu is a combination of blue skies, lush mountains, fertile rain forests, and a palm-fringed river.

Suva, the largest city and port, and the capital of Fiji, is set on the southeastern shore. The Nausori Highlands is a spectacular mountainous region in the central part of the island. Viti Levu is the site of the country's highest mountain, Mount Tomanivi, and its longest river, the Rewa. Off the east coast of Viti Levu is a small island, Bau. Formerly the indigenous capital, Bau is still the residence of the high chiefs of Fiji. Kadavu, the third largest island in Fiji, is located 62 miles (100 km) south of Suva. Rotuma, a Polynesian island set 440 miles (708 km) to the north of Suva, also belongs to Fiji. It has an area of 18 square miles (47 square km).

REEFS

Coral reefs have existed for thousands of years. A coral consists of polyps, which are soft living organisms, and a hard calcium carbonate exoskeleton secreted by the polyps. It takes billions of polyps thousands of years to produce a few square miles of reef. Coral reefs are natural habitats to more than 25 percent of all marine life and are among the world's most fragile and endangered ecosystems. Many reefs around the world have been damaged by human activity. If undisturbed, the coral continues to build on itself and grow in size. Millions of polyps live on top of the limestone remains of former colonies, creating the massive reefs. The color and shape of the coral depend on a number of factors, including the amount of light the coral receives and the quality of the seawater.

The waters off Fiji are the sites of some of the most beautiful coral reefs in the world. In fact, Fiji has been called the Soft Coral Capital of the World by enthusiastic divers. There are three types of reefs in Fiji: "fringing" reefs along the coastline, "barrier" reefs separated from the coast by a lagoon, and "atoll" reefs, which are circular or horseshoe-shaped. The Great Astrolabe Reef, Rainbow Reef, Great Sea Reef, and the Argo Reef in the Lau Islands are among the most famous coral reefs in Fiji. A balancing act for the Fijian government is the protection of the precious reefs, while generating revenue from tourism and diving.

Vanua Levu, the second-largest island, is about half the size of Viti Levu. Its name means "Big Land," and it is the homeland of about 17 percent of the total population. Much less developed than its bigger neighbor, the island is rugged and is surrounded by an extensive system of coral reefs. Volcanic in origin, the island has few beaches. Wide geographical contrasts are seen between the different regions. The interior is wild and mountainous, for example, while the western district is arid and sunburned. The southern coast is notched by several wide bays fringed with palms. Vanua Levu used to be the center of the copra trade, but today sugar cultivation is the most important industry, and large cane fields can be seen on the dry western and northern coasts. Taveuni is a large island to the southeast of Vanua Levu. It is notable for Mount Uluigalau, which lies on the 180° meridian, and the indigenous *tagimaucia* flower, which grows only here.

The Lau Group is made up of 57 islands to the east of Vanua Levu. Although scattered over more than 43,243 square miles (112,000 square km), their total land area is only 188 square miles (487 square km). The islands in the southern part of the group are closer to Tonga than Suva, and they reflect quite a bit of their Polynesian endowment. Lakeba, a central island, is a meeting place between Fijians and Tongans, and serves as the traditional political center of the whole group.

The floating island, Waga-qele, in Vanua Levu. Legend claims that early Fijians fished in the sea from three large floating islands but tribes from across the mountains wanted two islands for themselves. No agreement was reached, however, so they blocked the channel, leaving a solitary island that floats from place to place, responding to the chants of priests.

Lomaiviti, or Central Fiji, consists of seven large volcanic islands and a few small ones east of Viti Levu. Ovalau is separated from Viti Levu by 10 miles (16 km) of shallow sea. Levuka, on Ovalau, was the capital of Fiji until 1882. Situated at the foot of a steep bluff, it cultivates the ambience of a 19th-century whaling town.

The Yasawa Group is a crescent-shaped chain of islands to the northwest of Viti Levu, consisting of 16 islands and numerous islets, all of volcanic origin. Since they are located on the leeside of Viti Levu, these small islands are dry and sunny all year round. As the Yasawas are only a hop away from Nadi by a fast catamaran, they have become favorites with backpackers.

CLIMATE

Fiji enjoys a tropical maritime climate tempered by the southeast trade winds from May to October. The country experiences very slight temperature variations between the seasons. Summer lasts from October to March, with daytime highs of 85°F (29°C) and high levels of humidity. Winter temperatures average 68°F (20°C). In general, temperatures are cooler at higher elevations, especially in the mountainous interior of the large islands. Most rain falls in the summer months. The average annual rainfall is 120 inches (305 centimeters). The western parts of the Fiji Islands receive virtually no rain from April to October.

Hurricane-damaged palm trees along a Fijian coast.

Destructive hurricanes often batter this archipelago. The months of November to April are dubbed the hurricane season. Hurricanes develop from low-pressure centers near the equator. They usually reach their full force in latitudes such as Fiji's. Nevertheless, very destructive hurricanes are rare in Fiji. On average, Fiji experiences about two cyclones—severe tropical hurricanes—a year, much lower than other islands in the region. When a cyclone does hit, though, the wreckage is extensive, with storms causing millions of dollars in damage to towns, agriculture, and the tourist industry. In 2008 cyclone Gene caused widespread flooding and the death of several people.

Green hilly farmlands in Fiji. Because it is surrounded by a vast expanse of sea, Fiji enjoys a stable tropical maritime climate throughout the year.

PEAKS AND RIVERS

The larger islands are notably mountainous, rising abruptly from the shore to impressive heights. Most of them are of volcanic origin, as shown by the massive volumes of volcanic sediments and limestone deposits found. The highest peak in the country is Mount Tomanivi on Viti Levu. Formerly called Mount Victoria, it towers at a height of 4,341 feet (1,323 meters). Several other mountains rise to more than 3,000 feet (914 m).

A river meanders through a farming community on Viti Levu, near Suva, the capital.

Fiji also has many waterways. The longest river is the Rewa on Viti Levu, navigable for 81 miles (130 km) from its mouth. Other rivers on Viti Levu include the Sigatoka and Ba. Vanua Levu also has many rivers, although they are not as long as those on Viti Levu. The largest is the Dreketi River.

FLORA

Common edible plants in Fiji include food staples such as cassava, taro, and breadfruit.

Almost half of Fiji's land area is still covered with rain forest. Forested areas are found mainly in the high plateau regions. Rain forest species include the *dakua* and *yaka*, which are durable woods used to make furniture. These species are becoming rarer, because replacement trees are not planted after excessive logging. There are several edible ferns in Fiji, known as *ota*. Another edible plant is the *nama,* or grape-weed, a seaweed that Fijians consider a delicacy.

TAGIMAUCIA

The tagimaucia *(Medinilla waterhousei) is one of Fiji's most beautiful wildflowers. Blooming in long, 12-inch (30-cm) bunches from late September to late December, the red flowers display a white interior with a small red center. They blossom on a thick green vine bearing large green leaves. The plant grows only on the banks of Lake Tagimaucia, high in the mountains of Taveuni, and all attempts at transplanting it have failed. One of the most interesting features of the* tagimaucia *is that it comes with a beautiful and moving legend.*

A woman and her young daughter lived on a hill in Taveuni. One day, the little girl was playing when she should have been helping her mother do the housework. Despite her mother's repeated requests, she kept on playing. At last the angry mother hit her with the broom and ordered her to go away and never come back. The brokenhearted little girl ran away, crying. With tears rolling down her cheeks, she darted into the forest, not knowing where she was going. Blinded by her tears, she stumbled into a climbing plant hanging from a tree and became entangled in its vines. Unable to break free, she sobbed bitterly. As the tears fell, they changed into tears of blood. When her tears touched the stem of the vine, they turned into beautiful blood-red flowers.

At last the girl stopped crying and managed to set herself free. She ran back home to find that her mother had forgiven her, and they lived happily together ever after. Since that day, lovely red flowers have bloomed on the tagimaucia *vine.*

The orange dove is a small, short-tailed fruit dove endemic (native) to the forests of Fiji.

Casuarina trees, pandanus, and coconut palms flourish in the dry coastal areas. Fiji has several species of pandanus, or screwpine, which are grown around villages. Screwpine leaves are used to thatch roofs and in weaving baskets and mats. Mangrove swamps cover the eastern coastlines, while dry grasslands are found in the western areas of the large islands. More than 3,000 species of plants have been identified, one-third of them are native to Fiji. The most famous is the fuchsialike *tagimaucia*, which grows on the high slopes of Taveuni. It has red and white petals and bright green vines and leaves. The national flower of Fiji is the hibiscus. Introduced from Africa, it is commonly used for decoration and food, and in making dyes and medicines.

FAUNA

Fiji has scant indigenous wildlife. Most species were introduced to the islands by the first seafaring settlers about 3,500 years ago. One of the more interesting creatures is the mongoose, a ferretlike animal that preys on rodents. Of the more than 60 species of birds, 23 are actually native to Fiji. The orange dove can be seen only on Taveuni. There are also six species of bats and a few remarkable lizards. The crested iguana is one of the rarest reptiles in Fiji. Discovered in the early 1980s on a tiny island off Vanua Levu, it is believed to have drifted from South America to Fiji. Some snakes also live in the Fijian archipelago. One of them, the banded sea krait, is three times more venomous than the Indian cobra. Marine life is varied and includes most species of tropical fish. The leatherback turtle, which can grow up to 7 feet (2 m), is a wholly protected species.

THE NEW AND OLD CAPITALS

Suva became the capital of Fiji in 1882, thanks to its wide harbor and fertile land. It is now the country's administrative and political center and its major port. In a century Suva has grown from 200 to more than 70,000 inhabitants, and the town is continually expanding. Much of today's waterfront sits on reclaimed land. Suva is a cosmopolitan city, with many churches, temples, mosques, and cultural centers. The University of the South Pacific and the fascinating Fiji Museum are located there.

Levuka, the first colonial capital of Fiji, teems with history and old world charm. Sandalwood traders settled there in 1806, making Levuka the first European settlement in Fiji. The town prospered throughout the 19th century as sailors, whalers, and planters came ashore. Before the capital was moved to Suva, Levuka was a wild and lawless place. Today Levuka is the site of many historical landmarks, including the Cession Site. A stone marks the spot where the deed granting Fiji to Britain was signed in 1874. The people of Levuka are mostly of mixed Fijian and European descent.

Vitu Levu is the only known home of the world's second-largest insect, the giant Fijian long-horned beetle, whose body can grow to about 6 inches (16 cm) long.

Suva and its suburbs are home to half the country's urban population. It is one of the South Pacific's largest and most sophisticated cities, affording wide educational and commercial opportunities.

HISTORY

A tribal dance in an early village in Viti Levu.

FIJIAN TRADITION CLAIMS THAT the country was established by the legendary chief Lutunasobasoba, who arrived from Lake Tanganyika in Africa in a great canoe called *Kaunitoni* and landed on Viti Levu at Vuda Point. From there, he and his followers moved inland and settled the whole island.

Although no evidence exists to substantiate this story, many Fijian clans claim to be descendants of the first chief. But evidence does point to the fact that Fijian settlement is ancient and sophisticated. In the course of more than 3,000 years, Fijian history sometimes has been mysteriously clouded and highly tumultuous at other times.

Melanesians who lived in Fiji, then known as the island of Rotuma, centuries ago.

THE EARLY INHABITANTS

The first human settlement in Fiji dates from around 1050 B.C. at Bourewa in southwest Viti Levu. Archaeological evidence indicates that the first settlers came from Papua, New Guinea. The early Fijians were Lapita people, so called after a style of pottery found in coastal locations on many Pacific islands. Originating from Southeast Asia, the Lapita people were seafarers who, 3,500 years ago, made their way quickly through Melanesia and the Solomon Islands and across the western Pacific to reach West Polynesia, which is Fiji, Tonga, and Samoa. They made intricate forms of pottery and were highly skilled in navigation and canoe building.

A second wave of settlers, from Melanesia, reached Fijian shores in about 500 B.C. As the population grew, the inhabitants moved farther inland and turned to agriculture. Soon after, the Lapita people seem to have disappeared from Fiji, or were absorbed into the new culture.

Around A.D. 1000, Polynesian peoples invaded from Tonga, resulting in large-scale wars. By the early 13th century, Fiji was a province of the Tongan Empire. A complex class society evolved within the tribes, each headed by a hereditary chief. Considered a spiritual being, a chief enjoyed absolute power over his subjects who lived in *mataqali* (mah-tang-GAH-lee), or extended family groups. Marriages between the tribes were a good way of making peace, but fierce tribal warfare was still very common.

These petroglyphs, dating to about 1000 B.C., were made by ancient Fijian ancestors.

THE WHITE MAN

The first reported sighting of Fiji by Western navigators was in 1643 by Dutchman Abel Tasman on his way to Indonesia. His descriptions of the treacherous Fijian waters kept others away for the next 130 years. In 1774 Captain James Cook visited the archipelago, stopping at Vatoa in the Lau Group. In 1789 Captain William Bligh passed between Viti Levu and Vanua Levu after the mutiny on the British merchant ship HMS *Bounty*. Although he was hotly pursued by the hostile indigenous people, he made detailed and accurate observations of the islands.

Not until the early 19th century did Europeans begin to show interest in Fiji. In 1804 a group of shipwrecked sailors discovered sandalwood on the southwest coast of Vanua Levu, and the forests of Fiji were quickly ravaged by the beachcombers, who were mainly from Australia. This popular scented wood was bought for $50 per cargo and sold to the Chinese for $20,000. Within 10 years all sandalwood resources were depleted. In the 1820s an aquatic animal, the bêche-de-mer, a type of sea cucumber, brought the traders back to the archipelago. By the 1830s Fiji was flooded with sailors from Australia, New Zealand, China, the United States, and Europe.

In return for processing bêche-de-mer for the foreigners, the Fijians gained access to tobacco, metal tools, clothes, and guns. The availability of modern weapons provoked havoc among the warlike Fijians. The local population was further decimated by diseases brought in by the white men. A measles epidemic, introduced by Fijian chiefs returning from an official visit to Australia, reduced the Fijian population by half in only a century.

English explorer and mariner James Cook. After meeting some Fijians in Tonga, Captain Cook described them as formidable warriors and fierce cannibals.

CANNIBALS!

By all accounts, the Fijian people were a savage and brutal lot. One of their most repugnant practices, reported by the early Europeans, was cannibalism. For many years the islands were called the Cannibal Isles, and this foreboding reputation kept many Europeans away from Fijian waters.

Cannibalism was practiced in Fiji from about 2,500 years ago until the late 19th century. Prisoners of war, women captured while fishing, and shipwrecked sailors were invariably eaten. The worst fate that could be dealt to a captured enemy was to eat him. Eating a person meant destroying their spirit. Dead bodies were usually consumed on the battlefield, but live prisoners were taken back to the village and sacrificed to the local war god before being cooked and eaten on the god's behalf. In some cases the victors' cruelty went so far as throwing the victims alive into the ovens, or making them watch their body parts being eaten, or even forcing them to eat some of their own parts themselves.

Ratu Udreudre, a 19th-century chief on Viti Levu, was reputed to have eaten 872 victims. To keep track, he would add one stone to a big pile for each person eaten. According to his son, he never shared any of his victims, setting aside the prime human flesh in a box so as not to lose any.

Among the more often told cannibal stories is that of the Reverend Thomas Baker. The Wesleyan Methodist missionary, whose task was to convert the people of Viti Levu, unfortunately offended the highlands people and was killed in July 1867. His flesh was shared among the neighboring villages and eaten. The only thing remaining of the missionary was a shoe, which is now exhibited in the Fiji Museum.

TRIBAL WARS

By the end of the 18th century, Fiji was divided into half a dozen small kingdoms. Firearms and the help of white men, especially the Swedish adventurer Charles Savage, who arrived in 1808, favored the rise of Bau as the most powerful tribe. Although Bau is a tiny island off the coast of Viti Levu, it dominated western Fiji by the 1850s. Its chief, Ratu Seru Epenisa Cakobau, led a confederation of tribes and proclaimed himself king of Fiji.

In 1858 Cakobau proposed that Fiji become a protectorate of Great Britain when Fiji came under pressure from the American government to pay an unjust $44,000 indemnity. The American consul, John Brown Williams, had accidentally set fire to his trading post in a spirited Fourth of July celebration. Because he had leased the buildings from the Fijian government, he insisted that the government pay him damages. He was backed by his government, for the United States was looking for ways to exert some influence on Fiji.

The site of Cession Stone is the spot where the papers of cession were signed in 1874, and Fiji became a British colony.

When Cakobau came to realize in 1862 that he was not up to the task of governing Fiji, he offered to cede the country to Great Britain. His offer was rejected, and the Fijian chiefs organized themselves into their own confederation. This arrangement could not withstand the deep rivalry between Cakobau and his enemy Prince Enele Ma'afu, ruler of eastern Fiji, and the confederation fell apart in 1867. A Fijian government was finally established in 1871, and Cakobau was crowned king. Two years later his government collapsed, and Fiji fell into economic chaos. In 1874 a second offer of cession to Great Britain was made, and this time it was accepted.

BRITISH COLONY

Fiji became a British colony on October 10, 1874. The first governor, Sir Arthur Gordon, felt responsible for the protection of the rights of the indigenous people and decreed that all communal land could not be sold. He also instituted an administration that retained the traditional tribal chiefs system. As the Fijian economy lay in tatters, the governor undertook the cultivation of sugarcane as a cash crop. The Fijian population, however, was reluctant to work on the large plantations belonging to foreigners, so Gordon imported boatloads of indentured labor from India. This makeshift decision shaped Fijian history and politics thereafter. Between 1879 and 1916 more than 60,000 Indians arrived in Fiji. The indentured laborers signed five-year contracts. If they agreed to stay another five years, they were allowed to lease small plots of land in the second half of their stay, while still working on the plantations. Two-thirds of these workers did not return to India at the end of their contracts. As no land was available for them to buy, many set up small businesses. Although the Indians themselves decided to remain in Fiji, they resented their lack of rights and thus felt less loyalty to the country than did the indigenous Fijians.

Levuka in 1874. Soon after Fiji became a British colony that year, the capital was moved from Levuka to Suva.

THE WORLD WARS

As a British colony, Fiji sent about 700 European residents and 100 native islanders to fight in Europe in World War I. At the same time, a Fijian named Apolosi Ranawai started the Fiji Company, a movement aimed at stopping colonial exploitation by the whites. A commoner, Ranawai questioned the inherent powers of the chief system, which made this exploitation possible. Nevertheless, after being accused of sedition, Ranawai was exiled.

Fijian soldiers distinguished themselves during World War II in the Solomon Islands. More than 8,000 indigenous Fijians fought alongside the Allies in the Pacific. Virtually no Indians signed up because their demand for the same wages as paid to the Europeans was not met. For this reason, the Indian community was considered disloyal and unpatriotic. Fijian soldiers were so good at jungle warfare that they were never alleged "missing in action" if they could not be found. Instead, the phrase "not yet arrived" was used because it was actually likely that the missing soldiers would eventually turn up.

INDEPENDENCE

Although the right to vote was granted to white women and indigenous Fijians in 1963, the Indian community still faced discrimination. Having witnessed the successful struggle for independence in other British colonies in Asia and Africa, Indians started to call for independence, as they viewed the British to be the cause of their second-class status. The Fijians were less enthusiastic. Nevertheless, Fiji attained independence on October 10, 1970, exactly 96 years after becoming a colony. By then the Indian and Fijian populations were about equal in size. A number of Chinese and other Pacific Islanders had also put down roots in Fiji. The new Fijian constitution followed the British model of two parliamentary houses: a senate composed of Fijian chiefs and a house of representatives. Fiji also became a member of the British Commonwealth of Nations. Although the Indians did not get the full rights they demanded, they agreed to a system of communal voting.

The first post-independence elections were held in 1972, and Ratu Sir Kamisese Mara, a hereditary chief, became the first ethnic Fijian prime minister. His Alliance Party, composed of Fijians, Chinese, Europeans, and some Indians, stayed in power until 1987. Although Fiji was an independent nation, the sovereign was still the king or queen of England, represented in the country by a governor-general. The first Fijian governor-general, appointed in 1973, was Ratu George Cakobau, the great-grandson of the leader who had ceded the country to Britain. Fijian politics at the time of independence was still dominated by the chief-led clans.

THE 1987 COUPS D'ÉTAT

The 1987 elections were won by a coalition of Indian and Fijian parties that enjoyed strong support from the labor unions. Although 19 of the 28 coalition representatives were Indian, all cabinet positions of vital Fijian interest went to Fijians, and the new prime minister, Dr. Timoci Bavadra, was also a Fijian. The new government immediately set about turning Fiji into a truly multiracial and democratic country, disregarding racist institutions and trimming away the power of hereditary chiefdoms. Faced with the loss of their privileges and financial benefits, the chiefs convinced the Fijian population to believe that the government was pro-Indian and would take away their land rights. Demonstrations and massive disorder marked the first month of the new government. Indians were attacked in the streets, and government offices in Suva were fire-bombed.

On May 14, one month after the 1987 elections, Lieutenant Colonel Sitiveni Rabuka, a commoner, led a group of army officers into parliament and arrested the government leaders. He set up a new government consisting of old-timers from the Alliance Party and pronounced the governor-general, Ratu Sir Penaia Ganilau, head of state. Rabuka wanted new policies that would entrench Fijian domination in the constitution, and so Ratu Ganilau tried to work out a compromise to maintain civilian rule until the next elections.

Because Rabuka was not satisfied with the way things were turning out, he staged a second coup in September 1987. This time he declared Fiji a republic and proclaimed himself head of state. His new council of ministers was made up of powerful landowners and military officers. In October 1987 Fiji was expelled from the British Commonwealth. Ratu Mara, the chief who had become prime minister in 1972, came back as prime minister again in December, and Ratu Ganilau became the first Fijian president. Rabuka, the activist army officer, was named minister of home affairs.

RABUKA

Sitiveni Ligamamada Rabuka was born September 13, 1948. He joined the army in 1968 and had attained the rank of lieutenant colonel when he launched his two coups d'état in 1987. Rabuka was a dedicated soldier who had served in various peacekeeping missions. An ambitious army officer, he felt his career was stagnating.

A devout Christian, Rabuka is also extremely nationalistic. For him, Fiji belongs to the Fijians. His view of the Indian community in Fiji is highly prejudicial: because Indians are not Christians, they cannot be trusted. A lay preacher, Rabuka believes that Christianity is the foundation of Fijian society. If Indians were to convert to Christianity, he would welcome them with open arms. Although he is not a chief himself, Rabuka strongly believes in the traditional chiefs system. He sees himself as a warrior for his chief. His job is to protect his clan and bring glory to his chief.

Many political observers have argued that Rabuka was a pawn in the grip of various factions when he staged his coups. The most accepted version was that his first coup was masterminded by the American Central Intelligence Agency (CIA). The coalition government of Dr. Bavadra had announced the banning of nuclear ships from Fiji, with special emphasis on a nuclear-free Pacific. This was not welcomed by the American government, which sees nuclear engagement in the Pacific as vital for its own defense. Before the first coup in May 1987, Rabuka held discussions with a former CIA deputy director, and that was taken as evidence of the involvement of the United States in the overthrow. Another theory pinpointed the influence of the Methodist Church, which wanted Fiji to be governed as a Christian fundamentalist state. Yet another version held that Rabuka had been used by the tribal chiefs to regain their privileges.

Rabuka was accused of instigating the 2000 coup and the attempted army mutiny in September 2000, and he was formally charged with mutiny in 2006. He was, nevertheless, found not guilty. He now occupies several roles in the country, ranging from life member of the Great Council of Chiefs to manager of the 2008 Pacific Islanders Rugby Team. The lifelong patriot became sixty-two years old in 2010.

Fiji's previous
prime minister,
Mahendra Chaudhry,

RETURN TO CIVILIAN GOVERNMENT

After promulgating a totally discriminatory constitution in 1990, while in office as home affairs minister, Sitiveni Rabuka, who had given up his military career to concentrate on politics, was elected prime minister in the 1992 elections. To repair damages to the economy and regain international acceptance, Rabuka softened his views after becoming prime minister and promised to reexamine Fijian policies.

In 1994 the parliament was dissolved, and a new general election was called. During the campaign, President Ratu Penaia Ganilau died, and the Great Council of Chiefs elected Ratu Mara in his place. Rabuka was reappointed prime minister.

A new constitution came into effect in July 1998, guaranteeing full rights to the Indians and equal rights to all races. The document also changed the name of the country from Sovereign Democratic Republic of Fiji to Republic of the Fiji Islands. All inhabitants are now known as Fiji Islanders, a title that was previously applied only to the indigenous population. The new constitution created a human rights commission and established an elected, 71-member lower house of parliament. As a result of the new constitution, Fiji was readmitted to the British Commonwealth, and new elections were held in May 1999.

In the elections, Mahendra Chaudhry's Labor Party won an overwhelming number of seats, but in an attempt to appease Fijian nationalistic sentiments, the new Indian prime minister nominated many Fijian ministers to his cabinet. This decision was seen as another move to prevent a repetition of the tragic events of 1987.

TURMOIL IN THE NEW MILLENIUM

In spite of the new leader's best intentions, Fijian nationalists could not be satisfied, and in May 2000 an armed group led by George Speight, a failed businessman, stormed Parliament and took the prime minister and most of his cabinet hostage. The army commander, Commodore Frank Bainimarama, quickly stepped in and declared martial law. The hostage crisis ended in July 2000, with Ratu Mara and Rabuka accusing each other of masterminding the coup. Later that month, the military transferred power to an interim government headed by Laisenia Qarase, who remained as caretaker prime minister until the general elections in August 2001. Qarase's party won the election, and the former prime minister, Mahendra Chaudhry, became the leader of the Opposition. Economic stability returned, but not for long.

In 2005 the government tried to introduce three controversial bills, of which the Reconciliation, Tolerance, and Unity (RTU) Bill was most strongly opposed. Under the guise of national reconciliation, this bill was intended to pardon the perpetrators of all the preceding coups, some of whom, at that time, were members of the government. The RTU Bill stirred up a heated friction between the government and the army, which ignited after the elections of 2006 when Bainimarama called for the resignation of the Qarase government if it failed to withdraw all controversial legislation.

On December 5, 2006, Fiji endured its fourth coup in two decades when the army chief announced on national television that the Fijian military was taking control of the country. The takeover was swift and largely peaceful, with little disruption to daily life except for some roadblocks. Foreign governments, especially Australia and New Zealand, immediately condemned the coup, and Fiji was again suspended from the Commonwealth. Financial aid from the West, especially the United States and the European Union (EU), was also withheld.

In 2007 Frank Bainimarama was appointed interim prime minister by President Ratu Josefa Iloilo, a designation that was criticized by various sectors in Fiji. The interim government then started negotiations with the EU and other donor countries for the resumption of aid to Fiji. This culminated in an undertaking by Bainimarama to hold democratic elections by March 2009. In his 2009 New Year message, however, the interim prime minister announced that elections would be held only after reforms had been made to the electoral process. Later that year he conceded that the elections would not be held in 2009 but definitely "by September 2014."

A Suva townsman paints a protest sign on his house after the proposed military coup deadline passed in 2006.

"(The 2006 coup) was about rescuing a young and fragile nation that was being plunged into abyss and darkness by political leaders who were manipulative, frequently flaunted the law, and openly encouraged corruption and divisive policies to promote racism to suit their own agenda and needs."–Commodore Frank Bainimarama, 2006

GOVERNMENT

A guard stands vigilantly outside Government House.

CHAPTER 3

B EFORE THE MAY 1987 COUP FIJI was a member of the Commonwealth and a parliamentary democracy, with the British monarch as head of state. After the second coup, in September, the Fijian government became a blend of an English-style parliamentary system and Fijian hereditary rule.

Fiji's maverick military commander, Commodore Voreqe Bainimarama (at podium), announcing in December 2006 that Fiji's military had ousted the government. He dismissed the newly elected Laisenia Qarase and seized control of the country, marking the fourth coup in the troubled Pacific nation since 1987.

GREAT COUNCIL OF CHIEFS

Although Fiji has changed to a Western-style government, the hereditary chiefs still wield profound influence and power over the destiny of the country. Consisting of 55 members, the Great Council of Chiefs is made up of nominated chiefs from the provincial councils as well as the prime minister, president, vice president, and the minister for Fijian Affairs, who are automatic members. In addition to appointing the president of the republic and advising the latter on governmental appointments, the council also has authority over any legislation relating to land ownership and common rights. Council meetings are chaired by the Fijian Affairs minister.

In a strictly hereditary society like Fiji, the chiefs have never lost their authority, despite nearly a century of British rule and four decades of independence. Most of the high offices in the Fijian government and judiciary are held by chiefs from the indigenous clans. The Fijian governors-general and presidents have all been hereditary chiefs. The title "Ratu," used by the present president, is one of the titles conferred on traditional chiefs. One notable exception is Sitiveni Rabuka, who is not a chief himself but is now a life member of the council.

The Great Council of Chiefs was suspended by the prime minister, Frank Bainimarama, in 2007 and it remains dormant.

The 1990 constitution barred non-Fijians from access to the highest offices in the land. It also gave more power to the traditional Fijian chiefs. On the heels of international disapproval and in a bid for wider acceptance in the South Pacific, the Fijian government enacted a new constitution in 1997 that lifted racial barriers to political participation. This new constitution, which ensures representation of all racial groups in the government, came into effect July 27, 1998. The first elections under this more inclusive constitution took place in May 1999. Regrettably, the constitution was abrogated in April 2009, and Fiji currently lives under military rule.

REGIONAL GOVERNMENT

The Fijian archipelago is divided into four administrative divisions: Northern (includes Vanua Levu, Taveuni, Rabi, and other islands to the north of the

Koro Sea), Eastern (the Lau Group, Lomaiviti Group, Kadavu, Ovalau, and other islands in the Koro Sea), Central (the southeastern part of Viti Levu), and Western (the rest of Viti Levu, the Yasawa Group, and other islands to the west of Viti Levu). Each division is headed by a commissioner, who is assisted by a number of district officers.

The four divisions are further divided into 14 provinces. The provinces are administered by a council headed by a high chief. Provinces are broken up into districts, which consist of a number of villages. The village head is a chief appointed by the village elders.

The island of Rabi, with a population of Banabans, a Micronesian people, is governed by an island council elected every four years. The Polynesian island of Rotuma, officially a dependency, is also self-administered. Its council is headed by a district officer, seven chiefs, and seven elected village representatives, as well as the most senior medical officer and the most senior agricultural officer.

The Great Council of Chiefs is also known as the Bose Levu Vakaturaga (BOH-say LAY-voo vah-KAH-too-RAH-gah).

Electoral officials guarding sealed ballot boxes as they wait for voters in the May 2006 elections.

An interior chamber of Fiji's parliament in the capital city, Suva.

THE FIJIAN PARLIAMENT

Under the constitution of 1997, the Fijian parliament consists of two houses: the Senate, or upper house, and the House of Representatives, or lower house. Of the 32 seats in the Senate, 14 are appointed by the president on the advice of the Great Council of Chiefs, 9 on the prime minister's advice, 8 on the opposition leader's advice, and 1 on the Council of Rotuma's advice.

The House of Representatives consists of 71 members elected for a period of five years. To make sure that all communities are represented, 23 seats are reserved for indigenous Fijians, 19 for Indians, 1 for Rotumans, and 3 for general electors. The rest are open seats.

THE LEGISLATIVE STRUCTURE

The head of state of the Republic of the Fiji Islands is the president. Appointed by the Council of Chiefs in consultation with the prime minister, the president is also the commander in chief of the military forces. The

Fijian president serves for a period of 5 years, after which he can be reappointed for another 5 years. The maximum period of appointment is two full terms, 10 years.

The prime minister is in charge of the government. He is chosen by the president from among the elected representatives as the best person to lead the country, regardless of racial background. This usually means the leader of the party holding the largest number of seats in parliament.

The prime minister names a cabinet of ministers to help him in his task of governing the country. This cabinet, according to the constitution, must include members of the various parties seated in the House of Representatives. Every party with more than 8 members in parliament must be offered a proportionate number of cabinet posts. At present, the interim government cabinet is made up of 15 ministers.

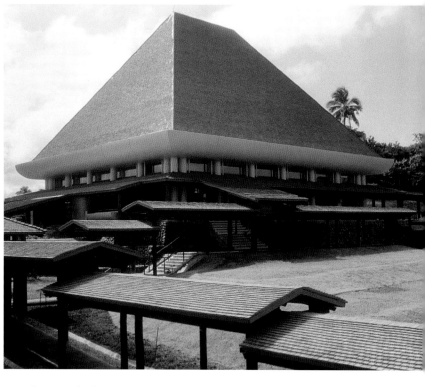

The Fijian Parliament Building in Suva reflects Fiji's cultural history.

NATIONAL DEFENSE

The Republic of Fiji Military Forces (RFMF) is responsible for the defense of the whole archipelago and the surveillance of the country's territorial waters. The RFMF has about 4,000 well-trained personnel who also take part in building projects and are trained in basic trades. The RFMF regularly deploys contingents to United Nations (UN) peacekeeping missions worldwide, and Fijian soldiers sometimes have the opportunity to train with officers from Australia, New Zealand, and Great Britain through several agreements among the countries. Fijian soldiers are excellent at jungle warfare. They served brilliantly with Allied forces in World War II.

Armed forces standing on parade at the Queen Elizabeth Barracks, Fiji's main army base, in Suva.

The RFMF Naval Squadron, formed in 1975, maintains Fiji's sovereignty at sea. The archipelago has declared a 200-mile (320-km) exclusive economic zone, and it is the responsibility of the Naval Squadron to conduct search-and-rescue operations in the area, and to ensure that no foreign ships are exploiting the marine or other resources in Fiji's exclusive economic zone.

THE JUDICIARY

The judiciary is an independent branch of the Fijian government. It consists of a system of courts, including the High Court, the Court of Appeal, and the Supreme Court. The powerful Supreme Court has the last word in any legal controversy.

The High Court includes the chief justice and up to 18 subordinate judges. It hears civil and criminal cases, with unlimited jurisdiction. The Court of Appeal consists of the president, who must be a judge, and a number of other judges, who may be High Court judges. The chief justice is also the president of the Court of Appeal. The Court of Appeal hears all appeals from judgments made by the High Court. The Supreme Court is made up of the chief justice, the members of the Court of Appeal, and other appointed judges.

The chief justice is appointed by the president on the advice of the prime minister after consultation with the leader of the opposition. Other judges

The Native Land Trust Board (NLTB) is responsible for protecting the rights and interests of native owners by reserving ample land for their needs and for providing suitable land for resettlement.

are appointed by the president on the recommendation of the Judicial Services Commission. All judges, including the chief justice, must step down when they reach the age of 70.

LAND RIGHTS

Aside from the 10 percent that was sold to Europeans and Australians prior to Fiji's cession to Great Britain, most of the land is owned by ethnic Fijians. Indigenous land is reserved for use by the 6,600 clans. Clans do not work the land communally. Rather, it is divided into lots, with each family receiving one lot. The owners can use it for agriculture or lease it for up to 30 years. This arrangement, however, has led to dissatisfaction. Owners are extremely frustrated that their land is being worked by outsiders at low rents, while tenants feel that they are at the mercy of owners who might not renew their leases.

The Fijian coat of arms has been in use since the day Fiji became an independent nation. The design of the flag was selected in a national competition to choose the country's emblem.

NATIONAL SYMBOLS

The background color of the Fijian flag is sky blue. In the top left corner stands the Union Jack, the flag of Great Britain, to denote the relationship between Fiji and its former colonial ruler. To the center right of the flag is a shield. Across the top of the shield is a yellow lion holding a cocoa pod in its forepaws. The lion represents Great Britain and the cocoa pod heralds the natural resources of Fiji. The shield itself is separated into four sections by the Cross of Saint George, the patron saint of England. Other symbols of Fijian agriculture in three sections of the crest are the three stalks of sugarcane, a coconut palm, and a bunch of bananas. In the last, bottom left section, is a dove of peace, the main feature of the Fijian flag before the country was ceded to Great Britain.

The Fijian coat of arms consists of two Fijian warriors holding on to the shield that appears on the flag. A stylized canoe stands above the shield, and below it is the motto of the Fijian people: *Revaka na Kalou ka Doka na Tui*. It means, Fear God and Honor the Queen.

ECONOMY

Sugarcane loaded on a truck in Nadi. This harvest will
be processed, refined, and exported internationally.

CHAPTER 4

T HE FIJIAN ECONOMY HAS MOVED from a nearly total dependence on sugarcane during colonial times to a more diversified one in recent years. Although agriculture is still an important part of the economy, light industries and the service sector are contributing a larger share of revenues.

In the wake of the coups d'état in 1987, Fiji experienced an 11 percent negative growth in gross domestic product (GDP), the Fijian dollar was devalued by more than 25 percent , and inflation shot up to 12 percent.

The largest city between Honolulu and Auckland, Suva, the capital of Fiji, wraps around a superb deepwater harbor and is a beacon of cosmopolitan office buildings.

By following strict guidelines laid down by the International Monetary Fund (IMF), the Fijian economy was able to recover within a decade. The 2006 coup, nevertheless, negated all this progress and created a difficult business climate, with the current account deficit reaching 23 percent of GDP in that year. In April 2009 the Reserve Bank of Fiji devalued the Fiji dollar by 20 percent in a bid to boost tourism earnings and export revenue. Consequently, foreign reserves reached F$700 million, compared with F$441 million before devaluation.

AGRICULTURE

Agriculture is still one of the driving forces of the Fijian economy, although it has been overtaken by tourism as the main foreign exchange earner. The largest sector of the economy, agriculture employs about half of the total workforce and produces more than a third of all exports. Crops are planted mostly on the drier western sides of Viti Levu and Vanua Levu.

Although sugar is still the mainstay of Fijian agriculture, the industry is in decline. Sugarcane cultivation is labor intensive, employing more than a quarter of the workforce, but with relatively low profit margins because of inefficient production methods. Sugarcane is planted by about 18,000 farmers on small plots rented for a period of 30 years from the government or from Fijian *mataqalis*, clan groups. Although most sugarcane planters are Indians, the Fijian presence is growing in the sector. After they have harvested the

A sugarcane field and colorful farmhouse by the Ba River.

cane, farmers sell their crops to the Fiji Sugar Corporation (FSC), which is a government-owned enterprise. A contract between the cultivators and the FSC sets the prices of the sugarcane and also assigns a quota for each farm. The FSC runs the mills that process the canes into sugar. There are three mills in Viti Levu and one in Vanua Levu. The sugar is exported via bulk sugar terminals situated at Lautoka (Viti Levu) and Malau (Vanua Levu).

A copra worker on Taveuni Island scooping coconut kernels before drying the coconut meat.

In the 1860s an Englishman bought a copra plantation in Savusavu from a local chief for 10 rifles. Some of today's nationalistic Fijians would like to buy it back–at the same price!

By-products of sugar include molasses, a thick dark syrup that remains after the sugar has solidified into crystals, from which rum and other liquors are made. It is also used in cooking and as cattle feed. Most of Fiji's sugar production is exported to Australia, New Zealand, Great Britain, and the European Union through a number of trade conventions. In the aftermath of the 2006 coup and because of World Trade Organization (WTO) rulings on free trade, Fijian sugar is under threat because it has lost the preferential rates extended by the EU. Moreover, calls for a sugar boycott have come from the EU environmental lobby in light of unsustainable practices in the industry.

Other agricultural products include copra and coconut oil, rice, root crops, and vegetables. These are mainly grown for local consumption. One sector that the government actively supports is the production of timber. About one-sixth of the total land area of Fiji is consigned to logging businesses, and the Ministry of Forestry has started a program of reforestation to supply the timber industry. Trees grown for the lumber industry are mainly mahogany and pine. Timber exports consist mainly of sawn logs, wood chips, plywood, and veneers. There is a ban, however, on the export of logs from indigenous trees.

To set the economy back on its feet after the disastrous post-coups years, the Fijian government set up the Fiji Trade and Investment Board (FTIB) to find foreign partners for local firms or to encourage foreigners to start companies in the country. The government favors partnerships with Fijians, since less money leaves the country, but businesses that meet the government's criteria can be 100 percent foreign-owned if the investor does not want a partnership. Priority is also given to those businesses that are export-oriented because they bring in much needed foreign exchange. Generous incentives include unrestricted movement of funds and profit repatriation, tax holidays, duty concessions on import of machinery, and the lifting of double taxation with certain countries.

Opportunities abound in the manufacturing sector. Aside from the long-established garment and footwear factories, which employ a large number of people with few skills, the Fijian government is pursuing investment in the electronics sector. Since there are only two plants developing and manufacturing electronic goods for export, this sector looks set for exponential growth. The goal is for Fiji to become a major player in the assembly of computers. Factories that export more than 95 percent of their output enjoy tax-free status. Incentives include exemption of customs duty on equipment and raw materials as well as waivers of licensing fees.

Moving along with the times, Fiji aims to become a major offshore center for information-exporting enterprises. With its English-speaking labor force and the advantage of its time difference with major business centers around the world, Fiji is ideally suited to provide telecommunication services such as call centers. A related sector is the information technology (IT) service industry, for which the country is seeking foreign investment to help its development.

Another sector where foreign money is actively sought is the tourism industry. Hotels import 80 percent of their purchases for food, linen, and glassware at concessional rates. They can also write off 55 percent of their set-up costs against taxes over a period of six years.

Looking ahead, to elicit the development of a more upscale type of tourism, the government has implemented an incentive package for five-star hotels. To qualify, a hotel must have a minimum of 200 rooms with a start-up investment of $40 million. The company will enjoy a 20-year tax holiday on all corporate taxes, reduced rates for electricity, and duty-free concessions on imported building materials.

The Fijian government is also promoting its beautiful country as an ideal location for shooting movies. Citing its breathtaking landscapes and modern amenities, it hopes to attract filmmakers from the United States and Asian countries. Deal-making exemptions on taxes and duties are among the incentives.

TOURISM

The strongest performer in the Fijian economy, tourism accounts for 15 percent of GDP. It is the largest money-earner, employing an estimated 40,000 people. About 58 percent of total revenues, however, are either repatriated by foreign investors—sent back to their home countries—or used to pay for tourism-related imports. Fiji is by far the most popular tourist destination in the South Pacific, attracting more than 500,000 visitors in 2008. Most tourists come from Australia, New Zealand, Japan, Britain, and the United States. Since the start of regular nonstop flights from Los Angeles in the mid-1990s, the number of American tourists to Fiji has increased steadily. Americans now make up about 12 percent of all arrivals.

Most tourists stay in large beach resorts on the west coast of Viti Levu. They are attracted by the warm weather, excellent diving, and duty-free shopping. The majority of hotels are owned by foreigners and managed by European hoteliers. Front-line jobs, such as tour guides and hotel clerks and managers, go to Fijians, while Indians fill the technical positions. The Fijian Visitors Bureau (FVB) is responsible for promoting tourism to the country, using media and goodwill activities.

A local staff member attending to tourists at an outdoor restaurant at the Sheraton Royal Denarau resort in Nadi. Fresh tropical dishes are very popular with visitors.

In a 2007 survey Fiji was voted as one of the top 10 most recognized names in the world, evoking romantic South Sea island images in respondents. Today, however, tourists, especially Australians and New Zealanders, are staying away from Fiji in droves because of the foreboding political situation. Hotel occupancy rates sit below 50 percent, with the luxury high-end resorts being hardest hit.

MINING

The only mineral that is exploited on an industrial scale is gold. A small amount of silver is also produced. The larger of the two gold mines is at Vatukoula in northern Viti Levu, with a labor force of about 1,000 men. Production has increased in recent years with the updating of mining equipment.

Extensive copper deposits have been found at Namosi, to the northwest of Suva, on Viti Levu. In January 2008 the Namosi Joint Venture (NJV) owned by Australian and Japanese investors, began to explore the area, and these investigations revealed that the metal was in fact of a higher grade than previously evalued. With the elevated prices of metals on the world markets, the Fijian government is eager to get the project underway. Namosi is targeted to become one of the largest mines in the world, catastrophically altering the landscape of Viti Levu and having wide-ranging impact on the lifestyle and environment of the local population.

A mechanic inspects the undercarriage of a vehicle used to bring ore from deep under the surface at Vatukoula Gold Mine in Viti Levu. Gold was first discovered in 1929 on Vanua Levu, and it spawned a mini gold rush that lasted into the mid-1930s. New material and technology has revitalized the industry.

FISHING

From being one of the early successes of the Fijian economy, the fisheries sector has run into some difficulties, but now is more stable. In the early 21st century, fish products accounted for nearly 10 percent of export revenue, with canned fish being the country's fourth-largest export. Most of the exported canned fish is tuna, but mackerel is also canned for the local market. The largest market for Fiji's canned tuna is the EU, while a large amount of refrigerated or iced yellowfin tuna is sent to the United States and Japan to be consumed as sashimi (raw fish). Other export products are trochus shell, shark's fins, and bêche-de-mer—sea cucumber.

Several companies are involved in tuna canning, including the Pacific Fishing Company (PAFCO), a government-owned company that runs a major fish processing plant at Levuka. One of the most active plants in the Pacific, it consistently and very efficiently produces high-quality fish both for export and local consumption. The challenges that lie ahead for the Fijian fishing industry are how to manage the depleting stocks of tuna as well as how to protect their resources from encroachment by foreign vessels. On the processing front, it is imperative for canning and associated companies to insist on uniformly high standards of hygiene and quality control.

The national market is supplied by local fishermen in small boats. Almost 1,500 boats are registered, manned by 3,500 crewmen. Nearly all the fishermen who supply fish on a large scale are men. Women are involved only in subsistence fishing—feeding the family.

TRADE

Fiji is an important center for regional trading. Imports have exceeded exports by more than 100 percent for many years. In 2008 total exports amounted to $750 million, while imports totaled $1.8 billion. Reexports—goods assembled in Fiji from imported raw materials, meant for export to other countries—were $250 million. These are mainly petroleum products sold to visiting aircraft and ships and to neighboring countries.

Merchant ships from many nations put in at Fiji's busy ports.

Fiji's main exports are raw sugar, garments, unrefined gold, bottled water, and canned fish. Major imports include manufactured goods, machinery and transportation equipment, fuels, and food. Fiji's major export markets are Australia, the United States, the EU, Japan, and New Zealand, while Singapore, Australia, New Zealand, Japan, and the United States are the main sources of imports.

TRANSPORTATION

Infrastructure is adequate in the larger islands. There are about 3,000 miles (4,827 km) of roads, of which 1,051 miles (1,692 km) are all-weather roads. Public transportation, such as the bus service, reaches most districts of the major islands, and taxis are readily available in the urban centers. Fares are fixed by the government. Many Fijians travel by "running cabs." They are shared taxis, and the fares depend on the number of passengers. Another cheap method of transportation is the truck. Passengers ride in the back of a small, hooded truck for a sometimes bumpy shared trip.

Most roads in Fiji are narrow, crooked, and poorly maintained. What is more, drivers have to contend with potholes, landslides, and stray animals (dogs, cows, and horses), all of which can be especially dangerous at night.

The Nadi
International
Airport in Fiji is
a hub to vast
transoceanic travel.

The Fijian international airport is at Nadi. An airport at Nausori handles regional and domestic interisland flights. The national carrier is Air Pacific, which flies to various remote destinations in the Pacific Ocean as well as Australia, New Zealand, Japan, and the United States. Domestic services are provided by Pacific Sun (the domestic arm of Air Pacific) and Pacific Islands Seaplanes, which operates planes that take off and land on water. Aside from the air services, interisland travel is supplied by a number of ferries and smaller craft.

FIJI WATER

As unlikely as it may seem, water has become one of the pillars of the Fijian economy. In 1996 the Fiji Water Company began bottling pure artesian water from a multimillion-dollar plant at Yaqara, in northern Viti Levu. The next year it started exporting its square bottles to the United States. The company now exports to many areas of the world as well, including Australia, Britain, Canada, the Caribbean, France, Germany, Mexico, and Spain—with total annual sales worth more than F$150 million. The bottling plant at Yaqara fills and sends out 50,000 bottles per hour.

Fiji Water is now the third-largest export item after sugar and fish, accounting for 20 percent of all exports and contributing 3 percent of GDP. In the United States it became the second-most popular bottled water after entertainment celebrities and politicians were spotted drinking it.

Fiji Water is pumped from an underground chamber deep beneath the Nakauvadra Range where it is protected by layers of soft rock and clay. It claims not only to be pure but also to contain high levels of minerals such as calcium, magnesium, and silica.

Ironically, despite the company's claim to be "green," it takes 5 liters of water to manufacture one 1-liter plastic bottle to contain Fiji Water. Taking into consideration the fossil fuels used in the manufacture of the bottles and the transportation of the bottled water to its major markets, as well as the carbon emissions during both processes, it is abundantly evident that the sale of Fiji Water is far from being environmentally friendly.

THE FIJI DOLLAR

The Fijian currency is the Fiji dollar. Its value is much lower than that of the United States dollar, causing imported goods to be very expensive for the ordinary Fiji Islander. Written as F$, the Fiji dollar was severely devalued after the coups in 1987 and again in April 2009. Although the devaluation caused great hardship for ordinary citizens, it also attracted many value-driven tourists and helped the country to earn valuable foreign currency.

Fiji dollars come in denominations of F$1, F$2, F$5, F$10, F$20, and F$50, while the coins are valued at F$1, 50 cents, 20 cents, 10 cents, 5 cents, 2 cents, and 1 cent. Although Fiji is now an independent republic, there are lingering traces of its colonial past in the Fijian currency: the portrait of Queen Elizabeth II of England still appears on some bills.

A local ferry transporting schoolchildren across Octopus Bay off Waya Island in the Yasawa Group of islands.

ENVIRONMENT

A gorgeous sunset at Nananu-i-Ra island, off the coast
of the main island of Viti Levu, in Ra Province.

CHAPTER 5

ALTHOUGH THE ENVIRONMENTAL degradation is not as serious in Fiji as in many other developing countries, countless practices, by both the local population and commercial enterprises, are a cause for concern. The major environmental issues today are deforestation, soil erosion, and pollution.

Soft corals and anthias fish in the reefs of Fiji. Beautiful reefs such as these are in peril due to widespread marine pollution from developing industries.

Since independence, more than 30 percent of forests have been wiped out by commercial interests. Soil erosion is brought about by inadequate agricultural methods and a change in rainfall patterns. But most serious of all is land and marine pollution. Rivers and the sea are polluted by pesticides and chemicals used in the sugar and fishing industries as well as the mindless dumping of domestic waste into the island waterways.

Recognizing the need to protect the environment, the Fijian government set up the National Trust of Fiji in 1970, a statutory body funded jointly by the government, independent donors, and multilateral projects, to provide for the protection of Fiji's natural, cultural, and national heritage. Fiji is also a signatory to several international treaties, including the Cartagena Protocol on Biosafety, the Convention on International Trade in Endangered Species, the Convention on Wetlands, and the Convention on Biological Diversity. Moreover, since 2009, the authorities have put into action the Environmental Management Act 2005, which aims to achieve sustainable use and development of natural resources.

Dumped domestic waste washes up on Fiji's fine beaches.

THE NATURAL ENVIRONMENT

Fiji's forests cover an area of 2.3 million acres (931,000 hectares) out of a total land mass of 4.5 million acres (1.82 million ha), most of them standing on communally owned native land. More than 40 percent of the forest cover remains intact, and some islands, such as Taveuni, still have contiguous forest stretching from the high-altitude cloud forest all the way down to the sea. The largest tract of virgin primary forest is the Sovi Basin on Viti Levu, which has become an important area for sustaining birdlife.

Three types of forest exist in Fiji: the tropical rain forest, the mangrove forest, and the dry forest growing on the leeward sides of the islands. Once covered with sandalwood, casuarinas, ironwood, and bamboo, the dry forest is steadily receding as the land is cleared for agriculture, such as sugarcane or pine plantations.

The rain forest is the habitat of 1,600 species of plants, 56 percent of which are endemic. Local hardwoods such as *kauvula* and *kandamu*, as well as the softer Fijian kauri, which is very common in furniture making, encompass the bulk of rain forest trees. The banyan tree is another beautiful, majestic feature of the forest. On the forest floor, elegant orchids and ferns grow extravagantly, while vines climb up to the canopy.

Mountains and a lush rain forest form a dramatic backdrop for Viti Levu Island.

Fiji's rain forest fauna is rather sparse in variety of mammals. The bulk of land-based species consists of reptiles and amphibians. Of note are Fiji's endemic frogs, which are terrestrial breeders, undergoing direct development. That is, tiny froglets or miniature frogs, rather than tadpoles, emerge from hatched eggs. Insects are more plentiful, with at least 44 varieties of butterflies. Birdlife is much more impressive, with 27 endemic species of land-based birds. These make up 46 percent of all land birds in the country. Flashy parrots, sleek pigeons, and long-tailed fantails create vivid patches of color in the forest.

The mangrove forest provides an important breeding ground for many of the reef fishes. Some 44,500 acres (18,000 ha) of mangrove buffer much of the coastline along Viti Levu and Vanua Levu, protecting the shore from the impact of hurricanes and wave erosion. Here, among the thick root tentacles, mangrove herons, kingfishers, lorries, and orange-breasted honeyeaters abound, as well as shrimp, small fish, and mud crabs.

Mangrove forests such as this on the lower Navua River harbor mud lobsters, herons, harrier hawks, and other wildlife.

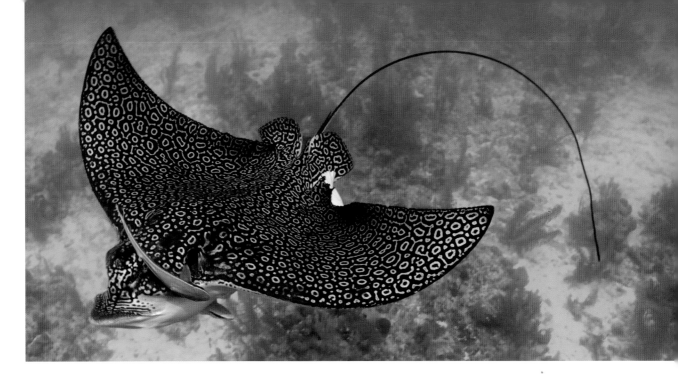

MARINE LIFE

The most distinctive aspect of underwater Fiji is the 3,900 square miles (10,100 square km) of coral that twist and turn around every island. Fiji's reefs make up 4 percent of the world's total area of coral reefs. Providing a natural habitat for thousands of species of plants, fish, and other animals, these amazing structures are comparable to the rain forests in terms of biodiversity. More than 600 species of coral live in Fijian waters—10 times the number found in the Caribbean Sea. Soft coral thrives in clear water less than 50 yards (46 m) deep, with an ideal temperature between 75°F and 85°F (24°C and 29°C). Thus, the slightest imbalance causes the reef to die, leading to dire consequences for the varieties of wildlife that make their homes among the corals.

The most colorful coral inhabitants are the reef fishes that make underwater Fiji look like a giant tropical aquarium. More than 1,000 species have been identified, with clown anemonefish, or clownfish, being most prolific. Equally ubiquitous is the damselfish, which comes in a variety of colors. Larger species, including grouper and barracuda, are less colorful. Of the three types of rays present in Fiji waters, the manta ray likes to bury itself in the sandy bottom of a lagoon. The rarest is the beautiful spotted eagle ray, which prefers to hunt in the open ocean.

Spotted eagle rays are excellent swimmers. Compared with other rays, they have long tails and well-defined bodies.

The Fiji crested iguana has experienced several local extinctions in the recent past due to extensive destruction of its habitat.

Outside the reef, dolphins, sharks, and whales patrol the seas, sometimes coming into a lagoon to hunt. Two types of dolphin swim year-round in Fijian waters: spinner and bottlenose. They live in groups called pods, mainly around the Lomaiviti Islands. As for sharks, a dozen species are found in Fiji, the most common being the small reef sharks (blacktips and whitetips). Big sharks, such as hammerhead and tiger, prefer to remain along the outer edges of reefs. The aggressive bull shark, on the other hand, likes to lurk in the murky coastal waters and mangrove estuaries. Pilot whales can be seen quite frequently, while humpback whales migrate to the islands from June to October.

Three of the world's seven species of turtles return to nest on Fijian beaches. Between November and March, the green, hawksbill, and the endangered leatherback turtles make their way to the small coral islands of the Mamanucas to lay their eggs. Despite a national ban on turtle hunting, their numbers are still dwindling because the local population continues to catch them. Turtle meat is a choice delicacy for Fijians and is also an essential ingredient in some ceremonial feasting.

ENDANGERED SPECIES

As of 2001, the International Union for Conservation of Nature and Natural Resources (IUCN) had listed 4 species of mammal, 9 types of birds, 6 species of reptiles and 1 type of amphibian as being endangered in Fiji, as well as 64 species of plants.

Many reptiles are among the most endangered animals in Fiji. Critically imperiled, the Fiji crested iguana faces habitat destruction from logging activities as well as predation from introduced species such as the mongoose and feral cats. Nevertheless, conservation efforts are underway, with the

National Trust of Fiji Islands playing a principal role. In 1980 the National Trust of Fiji and the landowners of Yadua Taba Island agreed to make the fertile island a national sanctuary. Since then, research, captive breeding programs, and educational and awareness programs have been conducted in conjunction with the Taronga Zoo (Sydney, Australia), Kula Eco Park (Sigatoka, on Viti Levu), the University of the South Pacific, and other organizations. The Fijian Crested Iguana Species Recovery Plan 2009—12 is led by the National Trust of Fiji.

Three species of bats are on the endangered list. The most vulnerable to extinction is the Fijian flying fox. Because its habitat is restricted to the mountain cloud forest of Taveuni, it is one of the world's rarest creatures and Fiji's only endemic mammal. The other two are the Fiji blossom bat, the world's only long-tailed cave dwelling fruit bat, which is found only in Fiji and Vanuatu, and the Pacific sheath-tailed bat.

The Fiji petrel is on the critically endangered list, and it rarely has been sighted since its discovery in 1855. It is unique to the island of Gau and after 1984 was thought to be extinct. Its first-ever photograph was taken in May 2009 by an expedition organized by NatureFiji-MareqetiViti, and a recovery plan is currently underway with the communities on Gau. Another very rare bird is the red-throated lorikeet, which has not been sighted since 1993. It is feared to be extinct.

Among fish species, the humphead maori wrasse is fast declining in numbers, due to overfishing and its own natural slow growth. Although it is a protected species, the wrasse is popular in restaurants and during feasts. To catch the large wrasses, some unscrupulous fishermen have been known to squirt highly toxic sodium cyanide on them, threatening the life of the whole reef ecosystem. Several freshwater fish are also considered vulnerable, but as yet there is no legislation to protect them. The rarest of them all is the *redigobius*, a small recently discovered goby, which is so rare that it does not even have a common name.

The Fijian flying fox is one of the world's rarest mammals, and is Fiji's only endemic mammal. This bat was first discovered in the montane forest of Taveuni in 1976. Since then, only five have ever been captured.

NATURE RESERVES

The Fijian government has established six national parks, four of them on Viti Levu, as protected areas of outstanding natural beauty. Administered by the National Trust of Fiji, most of the parks are located in the interior and encompass large areas of rain forest. The exception is the Sigatoka Sand Dunes, Fiji's first national park and the most extensive dune complex in the Pacific. Spread over 1,600 acres (650 ha) to the southwest of Viti Levu, the parabolic—bowl-shaped—dunes were formed over millions of years through coastal erosion. In places, they can rise to a height of 260 feet (79 m). Half of the dunes, however, are unstable. The area can be explored on official trails. It was there the elaborate Lapita pottery was first discovered, pointing to 2,000 years of human settlement, and archaeological relics and human remains are still being uncovered. In 1999 the Fijian authorities submitted the Sigatoka Sand Dunes to be included in the UNESCO World Heritage List, but it has not yet been approved.

Located in the steep hills above Nadi and Lautoka, Koroyanitu Park is the only national heritage park on Viti Levu. It was established to preserve Fiji's only unlogged upland tropical montane forest and cloud forest in order to create revenue and employment for the inhabitants of the six villages found inside the park. The park is crossed by the Mount Evans range, which contains several peaks above 3,000 feet (915 m). The tallest is Mount Batilamu at 3,920 feet (1,195 m).

Beautiful and ancient sand dunes above the beach in Sigatoka Sand Dunes National Park.

LÄJEROTUMA INITIATIVE

The LäjeRotuma Initiative (LRI) is an outstanding example of how a segment of a society can take charge of its community to work for the betterment of everyone. Based on the island of Rotuma, LRI was established in February 2002 by a group of Rotuman young adults with a vision of empowering the island's communities to make informed decisions about sustainable management of their natural resources. This community-based environmental education and awareness program mainly targets the youth, encouraging them to join activities focused on preserving their unique island environment, thereby becoming more self-sufficient and confident. Support has come from all over, including AusAID, the British High Commission, Youth Ministry, and Global Green Grants Fund.

LRI was formed to teach Rotuman youth about the impact development imposes on the environment of the island. This is done primarily through environmental education classes in schools as well as annual coastal cleanups. Since 2007, the organization also runs an annual three-day ecocamp where schoolchildren take field trips to learn about beach profiling, bird-watching, trash auditing (sorting and recycling), and financial literacy, as well as traditional tribal arts and crafts. LRI trains young adults in both rural and urban Rotuma to spread the message of conservation among their communities. Looking forward, the group aims to build community resilience to climate change, to revive the use of the traditional canoe in the fishing industry, and to explore options for sustainable livelihoods.

LRI is also involved in surveys and scientific research. An ongoing effort is the Rotuma Coral Reef Conservation Project. Funded by the Global Coral Reef Monitoring Network and Vodafone Fiji Foundation, LRI volunteer divers spend a few days annually surveying the state of the coral reef around the island. At community gatherings, islanders are taught about the reef's ecology and good practice principles for fishermen. So successful is LRI that it now advises the Rotuma Council on matters of the environment.

Moving beyond its initial focus on the environment, LRI is maturing into a more comprehensive organization dedicated to preserving the Rotuman culture and way of life. Rako is an initiative established by LRI together with the Fiji Arts Council to research and revive many Rotuman art forms that have been falling into disuse. Aiming to nurture and promote artistic excellence, Rako provides a platform for many young artists to express themselves through traditional arts. LRI gives Rako the needed cultural footing and structural support to ensure that indigenous arts are implanted deeply in Rotuma heritage.

A visitor relaxes in the serene pool of the second of three waterfalls along a day hiking trail in the Bouma National Heritage Park on Taveuni Island.

Within the cool vastness of the park lies the Garden of the Sleeping Giant. Housing more than 2,000 varieties of orchids, this garden at one time belonged to the estate of the late Raymond Burr, TV's *Perry Mason* and *Ironside*. More than 22 bird species have been recorded in the park, including the goshawk, peregrine falcon, white-throated pigeon, barking pigeon, and masked shining parrot. The two other national parks on Viti Levu are the Nausori Highlands west of Nadi and Colo-i-Suva, just outside the capital.

The other national heritage park is Bouma, which takes up almost one-quarter of the island of Taveuni. Although it is called a national park, Bouma is actually privately owned and run by the people of Bouma district, who established the park in 1990 with assistance from the Fijian and New Zealand governments. This 58-square-mile (150-square-km) sanctuary is an important wildlife reserve, keeping safe an ancient rain forest laced with waterfalls and making a home for rare birds and plants. Bouma encompasses such diverse elements as the Waitabu Marine Park, a no-fishing zone with 298 species of hard coral and 1,200 species of reef fish; spectacular waterfalls; picturesque beaches along the Lavena Coastal Walk; De Voeux Peak, Fiji's third-highest, with its unique species of birds; and Lake Tagimaucia, habitat of Fiji's most famous flower, the *tagimaucia*.

Located on the island of Ovalau, the Lovoni Trail starts from just outside the historical capital of Levuka and wends its way across tropical mountains to the ancient village of Lovoni, which is crouched inside the crater of a volcano, in the center of the island.

ECOTOURISM

Since the mid-1990s, the government of Fiji has recognized the dangers of mass tourism to the environment and has made the promotion of ecotourism one of the cornerstones of its visitor policy. The Fiji Ecotourism Association

was formed in 1995, defining ecotourism as "a form of nature-based tourism which involves responsible travel to relatively undeveloped areas to foster an appreciation of nature and local cultures." National policy recognizes ecotourism as one component of sustainable development involving local participation. Complementing—not competing with—conventional tourism, ecotourism brings together various stakeholders, in particular small communities that can earn a living while making sustainable use of their natural resources.

Ecotourism takes several forms in Fiji. Many resorts have adopted environmentally friendly practices, such as installing water-treatment facilities and making use of local materials. They also educate their guests about natural conservation, especially of the marine environment, and invite them to take part in turtle rescue and coral management. Another component of ecotourism is provided by the national parks, which offer hiking, river rafting, and other adventure-based activities. The cultural part is achieved through village visits and home stays, where visitors can sample village life and take part in various activities, such as the traditional *yaqona* ceremony that marks special occasions.

The first Fijian resort to become a member of the International Ecotourism Society was Matava Resort on Kadavu. At this most environmentally friendly hotel in Fiji, all waste is either recycled, composted, used in the organic garden, or fed to the local pigs. Power is generated by solar panels, and rooms do not have air-conditioning or electric fans. Of course, the buildings are made with local materials, and hot water is available only in the shower, heated by propane burners.

An ecotourist and his guide gazing at a crystal-clear waterfall while hiking along the Wainikoroiluva River area, which threads through the Namosi Highlands' lush rain forest.

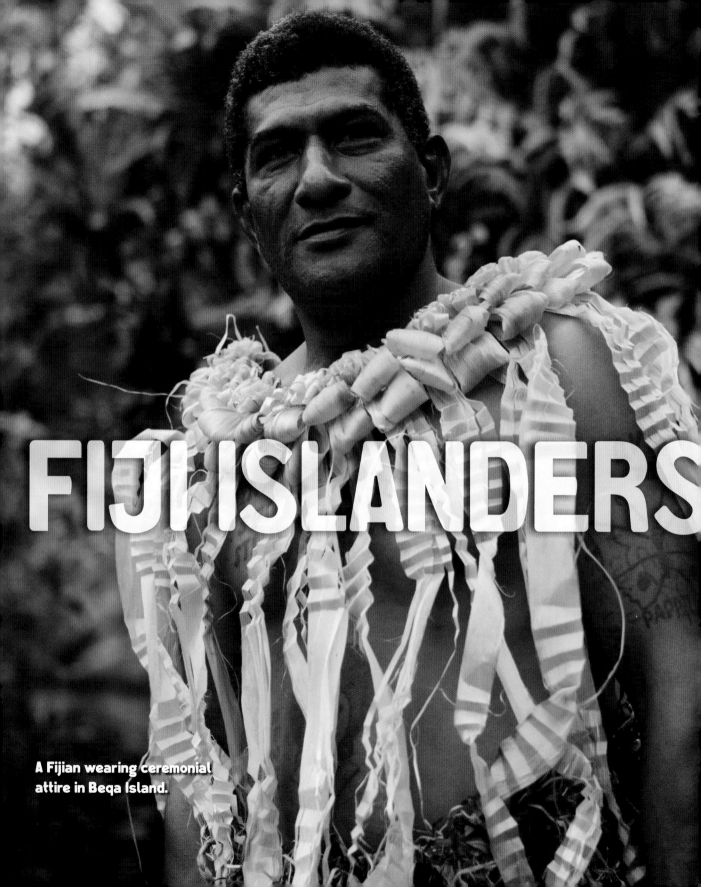

FIJI ISLANDERS

A Fijian wearing ceremonial attire in Beqa Island.

CHAPTER 6

N 2009 FIJI HAD AN estimated population of 944,720. Approximately 75 percent live in towns in Viti Levu, such as Nadi and Lautoka, and in the sugarcane-growing regions of Ba and Rewa. Vanua Levu supports 15 percent of the population, and the remaining 10 percent is scattered among more than 100 islands.

All inhabitants of the Fijian archipelago are called Fiji Islanders. Fiji has the most multicultural population of all South Pacific countries. Native

From a young age, Fijian children learn to be hospitable and friendly to visitors.

"A Fijian father, married to a European lady, of course their children qualify as Fijian. A Fijian mother, married to a Chinese or European or whatever, their children do not qualify as Fijian, if they are married. If they are not married, yes," said Stan Ritova, whose Fijian mother and part-American father are not married, so he qualifies to be a Fijian.

Fijians make up more than half of all inhabitants. The other large racial group is the Indian community, which accounts for 37.6 percent of the population. The rest is composed of Rotumans, Chinese, Europeans, and other Pacific Islanders, as well as those who are of mixed European and other origins.

The larger towns on Viti Levu are quite cosmopolitan in the makeup of their residents, while the smaller islands and villages are composed almost entirely of native Fijians. Indians predominate in areas where sugarcane is grown.

FIJIANS

The indigenous Fijians are of Austronesian stock and share a common ancestry with various peoples in Southeast Asia and Oceania. This diverse group of peoples inhabit almost half the globe, ranging from Madagascar in the Indian Ocean to Easter Island in the Pacific Ocean. Displaying a variety of physical characteristics, Fijians are related to both the Melanesians to the

A Fijian mother and her children. Although they do not openly express it, Fijian parents deeply love their children.

west and the Polynesians to the east. In general, Fijians are slightly less dark and are larger in stature than other Melanesians, especially Fijians living in the eastern islands. Those islanders in the interior and on the western side of Viti Levu, however, where close contact with Polynesians has been less frequent, are darker than their compatriots. Although Fiji is geographically situated in Melanesia, Fijian society has been most heavily influenced by the Polynesian chiefly system.

Fijians live in villages along the rivers or on the coast. Each led by a hereditary chief, these small communities can have anywhere between 50 and 400 residents. Indigenous Fijian villages are hard to come upon because they are always located far from the main roads. In western Viti Levu, villages are smaller still and social behavior is less rigid. An outstanding commoner who displays great leadership qualities can be elevated to the rank of high chief.

Most Fijian families are self-sustaining, growing their own food and making their own clothing. Although each family farms its own plot of land, communal

Traditional houses in a village in Navala, Viti Levu. Such settlements are hard to find as they are usually tucked away, by choice, from busy public areas.

life is very important. Fishing, village maintenance work, building new homes, and ceremonies are performed together as a group. Individuals are discouraged from rising above the community standard. Fijians who start a business are often stifled by the demands of their relatives. It is normal for Fijians to claim favors from those who are better off in the clan. This behavior is called *kerekere* (kay-reh-KAY-ray).

INDIANS

Most Indians in Fiji are descendants of the indentured laborers who were brought to work in the country's sugarcane fields by the British. The first Indians arrived in 1879 from the populous provinces of Bihar, Uttar Pradesh, and Bengal (today's Bangladesh). Subsequent arrivals came mainly from South India. They were dark-skinned, with straight black hair and black eyes. Although the system of indentured labor was abolished in 1919, Indians continued to migrate to Fiji until 1931. The later arrivals, mainly from northern Gujarat and Punjab, were wealthier. They came to set up trading businesses that catered to the large Indian community.

Indian chefs working at a restaurant, one of the many enterprises owned by Indians in Fiji.

Most of the indentured laborers chose to remain in Fiji at the end of their contracts. As they were not allowed to own land, many Indians invested their savings in businesses. Most village stores are owned by Indian storekeepers, who are very active in the retail sector. They continue to dominate the professions and commerce.

THE INDENTURE SYSTEM

When the British took control of Fiji, they resorted to Indian indentured labor to work in the sugarcane plantations they had set up. This system had worked well for them in Mauritius and Trinidad, and the governor-general had no doubt that it was the answer to a labor situation in Fiji. Negotiations with the Indian government started in 1878, and the first 450 laborers arrived in 1879. They were contracted for an initial period of five years, after which they were free to go home at their own expense. If they renewed their contracts for another five years, their return passage would be paid for them. In the first five years, the indentured laborers had to work exclusively for their employers, cutting canes for long hours a day. During the term of the second contract, they were allowed to lease small plots of land or to raise cattle.

Many Indians saw the system as a way to escape the famine and abject poverty of their home country. Others were hoodwinked into signing up. The labor agents misrepresented the distance between Fiji and India and painted a rosy picture of life on the plantations, with promises of wealth and great prospects. They also concealed the penalties for breaking their contracts. It was only when they arrived on the plantations that they discovered the reality. The laborers had to cut canes for 12 hours a day, and sometimes even longer, with only very short breaks for meals. Food was strictly rationed, and wages were low. If the laborer failed to complete the daily quota, his pay was cut and he was physically punished. Moreover, living conditions were terrible; the workers had to put up with overcrowding and no leisure. Essentially, the system was no better than slavery.

Despite the inhuman conditions, two-thirds of the laborers opted to stay in the country after their contracts had been fulfilled. For many of the lower-caste Indians, life in Fiji offered better prospects than in India, and many sent for their families. Between 1879 and 1916, about 2,000 Indians were transported to the archipelago each year, bringing the total to 60,537. When the system was abolished, some 40,000 Indians were living in Fiji.

In 1912 an Indian lawyer from Gujarat, Manilal Doctor, was sent by Mahatma Gandhi to look into the fate of Indian laborers in the British colonies. He arrived in Fiji after having witnessed the deplorable conditions in which Indians toiled in Mauritius. Calling for an end to this inhuman indenture system, he organized strikes and industrial labor action in Fiji. For this radical work, Manilal Doctor was deported from Fiji. Recruitment of indentured labor was brought to a stop in 1916, and the system was finally abolished in January 1919.

Although most of them have been in Fiji for four generations, the Indians have retained their ancestral beliefs and religions. Most marriages still take place within the same caste, although people from different castes interact freely in daily activities.

The Indian community is divided between Hindus (80 percent) and Muslims (15 percent), with a small fellowship of Christians. The Sikhs and Gujaratis, who did not belong to the indenture system, are considered elite. In general, Indians still associate more closely with other members of the same home province or dialect.

In 1986 Indians made up 48 percent of the population compared with 46 percent Fijians. The coups of 1987 provoked a mass exodus of Indians, and since then Indians have accounted for 80 percent of all migration from Fiji. According to official data, 100,000 Indians have left the country since 1987. Many Indian intellectuals and much Indian money left Fiji for Australia and the United States. Today Indians make up less than 40 percent of the population.

Many of the public transportation companies in Fiji are owned and run by Indians.

ROTUMANS

Situated about 289 miles (465 km) north of Fiji, Rotuma island became part of Fiji when it was ceded to Great Britain following wars between different factions on the island. The British decided that it was to be administered as part of the colony of Fiji, with a resident commissioner.

Rotumans form a distinct minority in Fiji because they remained fairly isolated from the other groups. Although they have been associated with Fiji for more than a century, they have kept their distinctive culture and language. Rotumans are gentle people who do not practice social class distinctions, although there are chiefs. Social life is based on kinship relationships and communal sharing.

The Rotuman population is growing fast, increasingly made up of children and youths. On Rotuma itself, however, the number of working-age people is very low, and elderly residents predominate. The Rotuman community in urban centers on other islands is well educated. Most of the males are employed in skilled occupations or the professions, while an equal number of women are divided between working and homemaking.

Rotumans in an earlier century. Of the 8,600 Rotumans in an 1986 census, more than 6,000 did not live on their home island of Rotuma but elsewhere in Fiji, particularly in Suva. Another 1,000 lived in Australia, New Zealand, and the United States.

Local residents waiting for a bus. Coming from different cultural backgrounds, Fijians have a multiethnic society.

BANABANS

Originally from Banaba (Ocean Island) in Kiribati, the Banabans were resettled on Rabi off the coast of Vanua Levu in 1942. This shift first occurred after their island was stripped bare by phosphate mining, and again when Japanese military forces invaded it during World War II. The island of Rabi was purchased with royalties paid to the Banaban population by the mining companies. In the 1970s the Banabans sued the British government and the British Phosphate Commission for compensation. With the money they were awarded, they established various companies and even built a new house for every couple getting married on the island. Lack of business acumen, sadly, led to the failure of all those ventures, and today the Banaban population is as poor as when it arrived on Rabi.

The Banaban population on Rabi numbers about 4,000, most of whom work in agriculture or fishing. The Banabans at first did not take well to life in Fiji. Many died from diseases because their bodies, accustomed to the equatorial heat of Banaba, could not get used to the lower temperatures in Fiji. Originally governed by a council of leaders, Rabi today is administered from Fiji through a Rabi Island Council. The Banaban administrators have set up various training programs for women and young people so that the community may become more self-reliant.

OTHERS

The rest of the Fijian population is made up of Chinese (4,700), Europeans (2,953), and part-Europeans (10,771), according to the 2007 census.

The Chinese in Fiji are descended mainly from settlers who arrived to start general stores or small businesses a century ago. Many originated in Southeast Asia, bringing with them their traditions. Today they are still prominent in the business and retail sectors and are generally well accepted by the Fijians. Many of them are wealthy merchants who have worked hard and prospered over the years. They tend to specialize in restaurant work and commerce. Although the Chinese have retained their language, customs, and religion, many of the Chinese today have married freely with the other racial groups. The local Chinese population is augmented by mainland Chinese who come to Fiji to operate truck farms.

The European community is composed of the descendants of Australians and New Zealanders who came to Fiji in the 19th century to set up or work on cotton, copra, or sugarcane plantations. Many of them married Fijian women to create today's part-European community. All of them are urban dwellers, and most of them are well educated and better off than native Fijians and Indians.

Children from different races are taught to live harmoniously with their multiracial friends and neighbors.

LIFESTYLE

A local woman navigating the typical mode of transport for Fijians, the bamboo raft or *billibilli*.

CHAPTER 7

FIJI HAS A LARGE URBANIZED population. Half of the total population lives in towns, especially Suva, which is becoming very crowded. Town life revolves around work or school during the week and church on weekends. Village life is more communal, with villagers getting together to share drinks or gossip in the evenings. Except in the towns, Fijians and Indians may live in the same neighborhoods but do not usually share the same living quarters.

After washing their clothing in the river, women spread the laundry out on bushes to dry.

Nevertheless, race relations are quite harmonious. Fijians and Indians work together amicably and freely interact socially. Some may even call one another "brother." Although a single national identity has not developed, the two races live side by side with tolerance, while retaining their ancestral customs and traditions. Perhaps the one truly national activity is the drinking of kava, a slightly intoxicating drink made from the dried roots of the pepper plant.

BULA!

Despite their scary past reputation as cannibals and fierce warriors, the Fijian people are very friendly and courteous. *Bula* (MBU-lah) is the most common expression of greeting among Fijians. More than a simple "hello," this word means "life." It is used to welcome guests, when meeting friends, or simply as a form of communication. Even though soft-spoken and rather reserved, Fijians greet each other with a smile and a cheerful "*Bula!*" or "Good morning." Except in the large towns, the same civility is extended to strangers. Fijians today enjoy a reputation for generous hospitality and warm friendliness, a stark contrast to the fear they aroused in visitors only a century ago.

A shopkeeper exhibits his wares in a market in Viti Levu.

FIJIAN ETIQUETTE

Fijian society is highly structured, with many social norms governing interactions. For harmony between neighbors, people talk softly and go about their daily activities with measured movements. Shouting or talking loudly is rude. Even small children do not run around screaming their heads off.

Since Fijian villages are private property, all visitors, including those from towns or other villages, have to obtain the headman's permission before entering. They should be bareheaded, as only the chief is allowed to wear a hat. Many restrictions apply to a Fijian's head. It is considered the most sacred part of the body, so it is extremely disrespectful to touch a person's head. Even patting children's heads is almost taboo. In the old days, anyone touching a chief's head, even by accident, was put to death.

Another set of rules governs a person's feet. Anyone entering a traditional Fijian house, or *bure* (MBOO-reh), must remove his or her shoes and leave them at the door. The person also has to stoop in a sign of respect to the owners and the people inside.

A young boy waves in greeting. When Fijians come across an acquaintance, they always stop for a few words. Just saying "*Bula*" is not enough.

CUSTOMS AND TRADITIONS

Fijians are very conservative and religious. They have, nonetheless, clung to many customs predating their conversion to Christianity. Some of the earlier practices, including tattooing and the circumcision of young girls and boys, have been abandoned. But many traditional communal activities are still alive. Several relate to fishing.

On Lakeba Island in the Lau Group, the villagers perform an annual shark-calling ritual in October or November. About a month before the event, the spot on the reef where the calling will take place is marked off so that no one

YAQONA CEREMONY

One of the most elaborate rituals in Fiji is the yaqona *(yang-GOH-nah) ceremony. It is performed with utmost gravity to mark births, marriages, deaths, official visits, or the installation of a new chief. Only traditional utensils are used: the* tanoa *(TAH-nwah) is a large wooden bowl in which the drink is mixed, and the* bilo *(MBIH-loh) is a cup made from half a coconut shell. A* yaqona *ceremony is full of pomp and ritual.*

All participants sit in a semicircle on a large woven mat in front of the tanoa. *A reddish cord decorated with cowry shells hangs from the front of the bowl, and is stretched toward the guest of honor or most important chief. Stepping over the cord is not allowed. The kava mixer and the kava server stand behind the* tanoa. *Women do not usually take part in the ceremony. When they do, they sit behind the men and are never offered the first drink unless they are the guest of honor.*

To prepare kava, the tanoa *is filled with water. Then the mixer places some powdered kava in a cloth, dips the cloth in the water, and gently massages it. The water slowly turns opaque brown as the drink is mixed. When the mixer thinks it is done, he fills a* bilo *and passes it to the guest of honor to taste. If the latter finds it acceptable, the mixer runs his hands around the* tanoa, *claps three times, and proclaims, "The kava is ready, my chief."*

Now the drinking proper starts. Squatting before the tanoa, *the mixer fills a cup and passes it to the server, who gives it to the first participant. The drinker claps once to receive the drink and downs the whole cup in one gulp. Everybody then claps three times, and the cup is passed back to the server. The same ritual takes place again until every participant has had his drink. When the bowl is empty, the mixer announces, "The bowl is empty, my chief," runs his hands around it again, and claps three times. This signifies the end of the ceremony. The whole ceremony unfolds in silence. A second bowl may be mixed and drunk, but with less solemnity. After the first bowl conversation is allowed.*

fishes or swims near it. On the designated day, the caller stands up to his neck in the water and starts chanting, which is believed to attract sharks. Popular belief holds that during the chanting, a school of sharks, led by a white shark, is lured to the spot. The villagers then move in to kill the sharks, except for the white one. The sharks are cooked and eaten later.

On another island, villagers catch a large type of mullet, a fish that is usually found in freshwater lakes. Once a year, clad in skirts made from leaves, the participants jump into the lake and stir up the water. This activity causes the fish to leap into the air, whereupon they are readily caught in the villagers' nets.

More commonly practiced throughout the islands is the fish drive. The whole village forms a large circle around the flat surface of a reef at rising tide. Holding a giant hoop made of vines and leaves, they slowly close the ring as the tide comes in, all the while singing, shouting, and beating the water with long poles. The fish are trapped in the circle and are easily driven toward a net near the shore.

One of the most solemn traditions is the presentation of the *tabua* (TAM-bwah). The *tabua* is a carefully shaped and polished whale tooth and is one of the most precious objects in Fiji. Once exchanged between chiefs as a sign of peace, today the *tabua* is presented as a sign of welcome or as a ceremonial prelude to doing business. In villages they are used in arranging marriages, expressing sympathy at funerals, asking for favors, or settling disputes. Fijians believe that *tabuas* are the dwellings of ancestor spirits and, if buried with the dead, will protect them on their own journey to the afterworld.

A Fijian man presents a *tabua*, a whale's tooth, to welcome guests to Fiji.

EDUCATION

Fiji has a good educational system, with a high literacy rate of 93.7 percent. Education is free and compulsory from primary to secondary levels, with the Ministry of Education overseeing all schools, most of which are run by

Schoolchildren ready for classes to begin.

local committees or religious groups. Thus Fijian schools tend to be of one race only, although the government has no policy of racial segregation in schools.

Almost all children attend primary and secondary schools. Primary school lasts six years. In the first three years the medium of instruction is the child's mother tongue. Fijian school kids are taught in the Bauan dialect, the dominant dialect in the country. Indian children are taught in either Hindi (for Hindus) or Urdu (for Muslims). The Chinese community also runs its own schools, while European children are taught in English. English becomes the main medium of instruction for everyone in the fourth year of school and beyond.

Secondary school lasts another six years. At the end of the sixth year, students take the Fiji School Leaving Certificate exam, which will sort out whether they go on to a tertiary or a vocational institution. Students can stay on for a seventh year and take the Fiji Seventh Form Exam. This is the equivalent of the freshman year in university.

Higher education is available at the University of the South Pacific in Suva. The USP is owned by 12 South Pacific countries, and there is another campus in Western Samoa, where the School of Agriculture is located. The Suva campus offers courses in the humanities, sciences, and economics. The university has more than 10,000 students, who come from most South Pacific nations, except for Papua New Guinea and the French and American territories. Established in 2005, the University of Fiji at Lautoka, Viti Levu, is strongest in business studies, the humanities, science and technology, and law. The Fiji Institute of Technology offers courses in engineering, commerce, design, and hospitality and tourism.

In addition, a number of technical and vocational institutions recruit those wishing to learn a trade or skill. Many of these institutions are run by religious affiliates, but the government has increased its investment in technical education, realizing its growing importance.

SOCIAL PROBLEMS

The main problem engaging the Fijian people is that of change. With modern development a breakdown of communal living overtakes many young Fijians who are looking for work in the large towns, in particular Suva. Without the traditional support of their village community, many young adults live confused lives and end up in the center of various social problems.

Migration from rural areas to urban centers has increased over the years, resulting in overcrowded conditions in towns. Unemployment, inadequate housing and educational facilities, and a rise in crime, especially thefts, can be attributed mostly to urban migration. Suva faces a serious housing problem, with a growing homeless population. Around 12.5 percent of the population of Fiji cannot afford adequate housing, living in substandard and unstable structures that are easily collapsed by hurricanes and earthquakes. In Suva alone, more than 28,000 families have to put up with such living conditions, cramming into small houses without the basic amenities. Those living in housing projects provided by the Housing Authority of Fiji do not fare much better. Although they have a sound roof over their heads and proper sanitation, they face the usual problems associated with such projects: crime, alcoholism, vandalism, and antisocial behavior. Domestic abuse, called "wife-bashing" in Fiji, is on the rise.

Alcoholism and gambling are fast becoming leading problems. With kava drinking deeply entrenched in the lifestyle of most Fiji Islanders, alcoholism is one of the scourges that the churches are struggling to contain. Lotteries are very popular in Fiji, and it is even possible to place bets on Australian horse races at betting shops in cities. Extreme betting dips into household cash.

Beggars using a box and umbrella to shelter them from the hot midday sun outside the Toorak Mosque in Suva.

"A hundred years of prodding by the British has failed to make the Fijians see why they should work for money."
–James A. Michener, *Return to Paradise*, 1951

HEALTH CARE

Fiji's population lives in generally good health, although the rise in alcoholism, sexually transmitted diseases, diabetes, and malnutrition is worrisome. These diseases are all linked with growing economic affluence and a changing diet, and the health authorities are trying their best to educate the population about them. The government is also concentrating on improving environmental health, such as providing better sanitation and an improved water supply.

Red Cross workers in Fiji participate in many humanitarian efforts and provide some basic health services, though not nearly enough in the impoverished system.

Health-care infrastructure in Fiji compares favorably with most Pacific Island states, with 70 percent of the population having access to health services. Only 40 percent of Fijians, however, receive quality health care. Inadequate health financing and a stark shortage of health-care workers hamper Fiji's primary health-care efforts. There is only one doctor for every 4,000 people and one nurse for every 500 people. At present, Fiji is plagued by a serious lack of doctors and nurses. Health care is provided by three national hospitals, 16 provincial hospitals, 75 health centers, and 88 nursing stations. In addition, there are two government-subsidized private hospitals, three specialist hospitals, and about 100 doctors in private practice. Health care is not provided free but is generally inexpensive.

FIJIAN DRESS

The traditional Fijian garment for both men and women is the *sulu* (SOO-loo), a wraparound skirt, or sarong. Traditionally made of *masi* (MAH-sih), or bark cloth, *sulus* are now made of industrial cotton. Men wear their *sulus* midcalf while women wear them down to the ankles. Formal or ceremonial occasions call for more geometric patterns and muted colors. A short *sulu* is part of the Fijian military uniform. Grass skirts are worn during traditional observations, such as *yaqona* ceremonies and dance performances for tourists. The costumes are made of plain dyed grass and feature flowers as ornaments.

Most Indian women wear the sari, both in town and rural areas. The outfit consists of a short blouse called a *choli* (CHOH-lih) and a long length of cloth wrapped around as a skirt, with one end draped over the left shoulder or the head. Muslim women and those of north Indian origin opt for a long-sleeved tunic over a pair of straight pants. Indian men rarely wear the traditional dhoti, or loincloth, except during religious ceremonies.

Most men in Fiji wear the *bula* shirt. Resembling the Hawaiian aloha shirt, the *bula* is made of cotton and comes in a variety of colors. Floral patterns are most common, especially the hibiscus.

Newlyweds, together with their bridesmaids and groomsmen, all dressed in the traditional Fijian *sulu* costume, with garlands made from flowers and bark.

RELIGION

The colorful and elaborate Sri Siva Subramanya Swami Temple is modeled after traditional South Indian Hindu temples.

FIJI IS THE ONLY COUNTRY in the Pacific where religions of the West and East meet face-to-face. The Fijian population has been Christian ever since the early missionaries managed to convert King Cakobau in the mid-19th century. Freedom of religion is guaranteed in the 1997 constitution, and Fijians recognize the main religions with public holidays.

Children at a joyful Sunday Mass in a Wakaya Island village church.

Fijian women today are treated with much more respect than their pre-Christianity sisters. In traditional Fijian religion, when a man died, his wife was strangled to accompany him to the afterlife.

The Indian population has retained its ancestral Hindu religion, making up 27.9 percent of all Fijians. Christians form 64.5 percent, Muslims 6.3 percent, and the rest consists of Sikhs 0.3 percent and others 0.3 percent. Only 0.8 percent of the whole population claims no religion at all.

The Fiji Islanders are very devout people, whatever their denomination. Every village or settlement, however small, has at least one church or temple. Religious activities form an integral part of the national lifestyle, and religious ceremonies are performed with the utmost reverence.

CHRISTIANITY

The largest religion by far in Fiji is Christianity. Almost all Fijians and 2 percent of Fiji Indians belong to a Christian denomination. The major denominations are Methodist and Roman Catholic. The Methodists are the most powerful among the Christian groups in Fiji, with more than three-quarters of Fijians

The Naiserslagi Catholic church in Viti Levu.

belonging to this denomination. Among smaller churches are the Anglicans, Presbyterians, and Seventh-day Adventists. The Mormons (Latter-day Saints) and other evangelical sects are newer arrivals who call on foreigners to disseminate their messages. With the Pacific Theological College and the Pacific Regional Seminary located in Suva, Fiji is a sort of Pacific Islands Bible Belt. The South Pacific is one of the few areas in the world where there is a surplus of ministers of religion.

The first missionaries from the London Missionary Society arrived in Fiji in the 1830s to make converts to Christianity and to preach against cannibalism. They did not

Christians singing during a church service at the village of Naidi in Vanua Levu.

have much success until it dawned on them that they had to convert the chiefs first. The first such conversion occurred in 1839 when a high chief adopted Christianity, together with all his villagers and the other minor chiefs under his influence. The turning point came in 1854 when Chief Cakobau realized that he had to become a Christian in order to secure the cooperation of the Christian king of Tonga. Many chiefs converted because they were impressed by the guns and machines of the Christian Europeans. Besides, the Christian concept of a supreme God was similar to the Fijians' own traditional ideas of divinity. Many Fijians continued to worship their own gods and ancestor spirits even after converting to Christianity.

Christianity is all-pervasive in the Fijian's lifestyle. Christians attend church religiously. Most people who attend the city churches dress up to go to Sunday Mass—women in white dresses and hats, and men in plain, long-sleeved shirts and dark pants. Church attendance is high, as all Sunday activities revolve around the church—the church service itself, Bible studies—and other community activities. At least one church or temple stands in each village or small town, and spiritual leaders are very influential and held in high esteem. Church choral singing is outstanding and fervent.

Hindus perform a fire-walking ritual as part of the process of spiritual cleansing. Generally practiced by Indians from southern India, this annual ritual takes place on a Sunday between May and September, to coincide with a full moon. For 10 days before the fire walking, participants remain isolated and eat only unspiced vegetarian meals. Rising early and going to sleep late, they spend their time praying and meditating. Spiritually readied at the end of the period, with their faces now smeared with yellow turmeric powder, they make their way to the sea or the nearest river for a bath. The priest chants selected prayers and pierces their cheeks, tongues, and bodies with metal skewers. Now in a trance, the fire walkers dance back to the temple grounds where the fire walking takes place.

Prior to the ceremony, a pit has been prepared with charred wood raked over glowing coals. Following the rhythm of chanting and frenetic drumming, each participant walks five times over the burning pit while being whipped by helpers. They feel no pain, and the soles of their feet do not get burned. Fire walking is the ultimate triumph of mind over body.

Native Fijians also have a fire-walking ceremony that is performed only by members of the Sawau tribe on Beqa Island, just off the south coast of Viti Levu. According to a tribal legend, a warrior was accorded the ability to walk on fire by a spirit-god that he had caught when fishing and then set free. Today the warrior's *descendants act as high priests during the ceremony. Just as with the Hindus, Fijians taking part in fire walking have to purify themselves. They abstain from sex and coconut for two weeks prior to the ceremony. They walk on heated stones, however, instead of hot embers. Only men are allowed to perform this native Fijian ceremony, while the Hindu fire walking is also done by women.*

The pit used is circular, with a diameter of 12 feet (3.7 m), and the stones are heated until they are white hot. The fire walkers psych themselves up in a nearby hut. Accompanied by much chanting, they come out and one by one briskly walk around the inside of the pit. After all of the men have had their solo turn, leaves and grass are thrown onto the stones, and all the walkers jump back inside the steaming pit while singing a farewell song.

Today fire walking in Fiji is performed mostly for tourists in resort hotels. The Fijian fire-walking ritual has lost all its spiritual significance and is not performed at all anymore on Beqa Island. As for the Hindu fire walking, many tour operators organize trips for tourists to watch it.

HINDUISM

The indentured Indian laborers brought Hinduism to Fiji. Hindus generally keep their worship to themselves and have not converted any native Fijians. As those who were shipped in to work in Fiji were all poor, lower-caste

Hindus worship with offerings of fruit, flowers, and camphor. Chanting and the beating of drums are used to acclaim the deity. Fasting and abstaining from meat are other means to get closer to the deity.

The Sri Siva Subramanya Swami Temple in Nadi.

laborers, knowledge of Hindu historical philosophy is at best fragmentary among Fijian Hindus. In general, wealthier Indians tend to be less religious.

Hindus believe in one supreme power, who takes on different forms and names in order to be understood. He can be both life-giving and destructive. The aim of the Hindu devotee is to appease the destructive manifestations while imploring favors from the life-giving ones. Hindus believe in serial reincarnation and that everyone will have to face the consequences of their past deeds. In order to break out of the cycle of reincarnations and attain nirvana, where pain and care are banished, they must lead a moral life. Their main path to holiness is through religious asceticism—austere self-denial. Most Hindu homes have a small shrine for family worship. Each Indian village has at least one temple, but there is no fixed day for worship.

A Fijian traditional high priest preparing a ceremonial fire.

FIJIAN FAITHS

Prior to the arrival of the Christian missionaries, Fijians believed in a cadre of gods and spirits that had to be appeased and thanked. Most spirits tended to be malevolent, and they had to be kept happy so that they would not vent their wrath on the people. Fijians also performed ancestor worship, and the souls of outstanding ancestors were morphed into local deities. Thus a war hero could become a god of war, while a successful farmer could become a god of plenty.

Chiefs and high priests were worshiped as representatives of the gods. Priests also served as the gods' mouthpieces. Idolatry took the form of worshipful attention to relics and carved whale teeth. The people offered food and kava roots for important rituals. Among their more barbaric practices were human sacrifice and mutilation.

Modern-day Fijians no longer practice their ancient faiths. But despite having been Christians for more than a century, traces of ancestor and spirit worship can still be found in their attitudes. The hereditary chiefs are still regarded as some sort of supernatural beings, although the Fijians have been taught that all humans are the same. The singing and enacting of rituals in church are other examples of the fusion of indigenous faiths with Christian practices.

A mosque in Sigatoka. Although Muslims are only a small fraction of the population, at least one small mosque can be found in every settlement.

OTHER RELIGIONS

The descendants of Indian immigrants, particularly the Gujarati traders from western India, Muslim followers of Islam believe in one God and follow the religious teachings of the Prophet Muhammad as set down in the Koran, the Muslim holy book. They are a conservative community who lead a strict lifestyle, with many dietary restrictions. One of these is a ban on the consumption of alcohol. Young Muslims in Fiji are more liberal, however, and some even enjoy a drink of kava from time to time.

Sikhs came from northern India. Believing in a combination of Hinduism and Islam, Sikh men are highly noticeable with their unshaved facial hair and turbans wound around their heads.

Buddhists are mainly Chinese. Worshiping Buddha, Buddhists believe in attaining enlightenment, a condition of immortality that will have put an end to all personal suffering. The Buddhists have a temple in Suva and run a few learning centers for Chinese children.

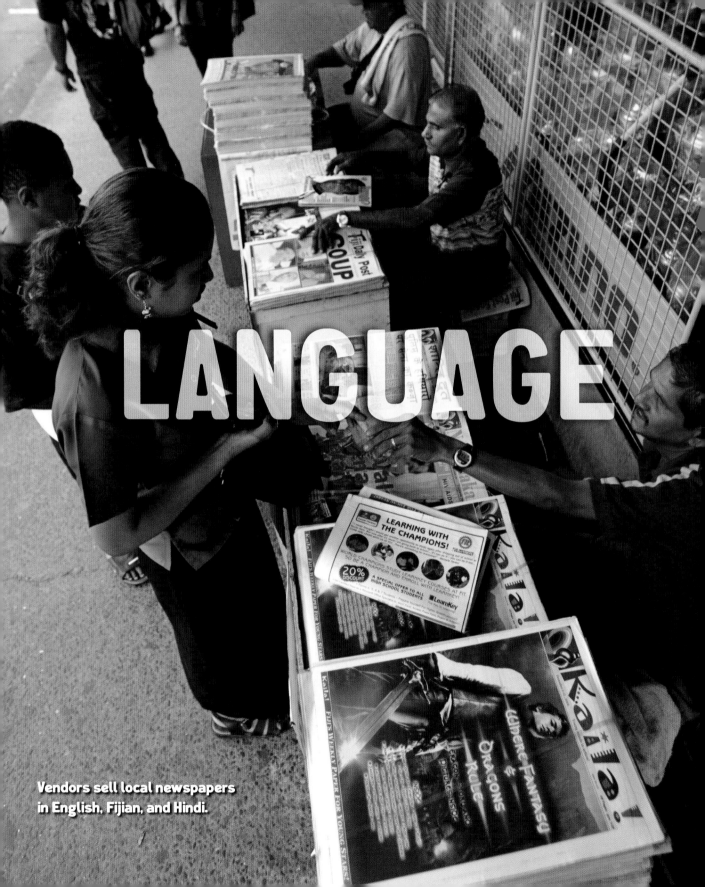

LANGUAGE

Vendors sell local newspapers in English, Fijian, and Hindi.

ALTHOUGH ENGLISH IS ONE of the official languages of Fiji, it is not the mother tongue of most Fiji Islanders. Almost everybody in Fiji is bilingual, or even trilingual. At home Fijians speak a dialect of the Fijian language, and Indians speak Hindi or Urdu. Nevertheless, everybody learns English at school, and all Fiji Islanders have at least a working knowledge of English. All official matters are conducted in English.

A young Fijian learning English by listening to audio books while also reading.

FIJIAN

The Fijian language belongs to the enormous Austronesian language family that spans half the globe. Fijian accounts for more speakers than any other indigenous language in the Pacific. Many languages in Polynesia—Tongan, Samoan, Hawaiian, and Tahitian—are historically related to Fijian. Fijian spelling, however, differs from the languages of its neighbors.

Out of more than 300 regional varieties spoken in Fiji, the Bauan dialect is regarded as the standard form of the language. In 1835 two Methodist missionaries, David Cargill and William Cross, devised a written form for the language, which until then had existed only in oral form. Cargill and Cross selected the Bauan dialect to represent the country because of the political and military supremacy of the island of Bau at that time. When they published a dictionary and a grammar, and translated the Bible into this dialect, the dominance of Bauan became entrenched. This is the dialect used in conversation by Fijians from different areas, in schools, and on the radio, and understood by all.

When Fiji was a British colony, the use of Fijian was discouraged by the authorities in favor of English, but the indigenous language reasserted itself after independence. The 1997 constitution established Fijian as an official

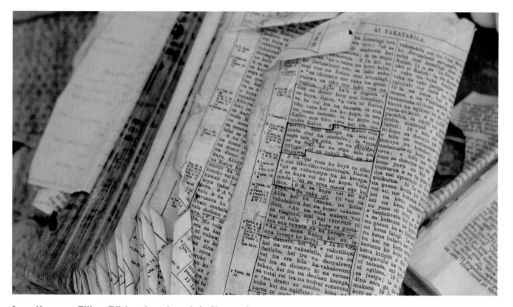

A well-worn Fijian Bible at a church in Vanua Levu.

language of the nation, and there have been calls in recent years for the elevation of its status to that of national language and to be made compulsory in schools.

HINDI

Hindi is the language spoken by all Indians in Fiji. Although Muslim immigrants used Urdu and South Indian immigrants spoke Tamil or Telegu, their descendants today all can converse in Hindi. Some Muslims may have retained Urdu as their household or primary school language, but they have adopted Hindi for practical reasons.

The Hindi heard in Fiji actually is not the pure form spoken in India. Rather it is a mixture of the various Indian dialects brought by the early immigrants. One of its main components is Bhojpuri, the dialect of Central India. Many English words, such as "room," "towel," and "airport," have also made their way into Fijian Hindi. Some words have taken on slightly different meanings, however. The noun "book," for example, also includes magazines and other forms of print. Understandably, no Fijian word is found in Hindi vocabulary. Hindi script does not use the roman alphabet but employs a set of symbols representing 42 different sounds. Indian children learn standard Hindi or Urdu in school, along with English.

Suva residents enjoy gathering at local cafés. The seated speaker is wearing a popular *bula* shirt.

Fijian spelling is still based on the orthography created in 1835 by missionaries Cargill and Cross. Some letters are pronounced differently from their English versions. Although consonants are always separated by a vowel, the actual pronunciation may involve two consonant sounds. Fijian has no pure b, c, or d sounds as in English. Vowels, however, are quite straightforward. Similar to other Pacific languages, the five vowels are pronounced in the same way as in Romance languages (such as Spanish or Italian). Each vowel is pronounced separately.

Vowels can be short or long. The longer form usually takes twice as long to say as the shorter vowel. The short forms are:

a as in "father"
e as in "bet"
i as in "machine"
o as in "occur"
u as in "zoo"

A long vowel can have a mark above it called a macron, as in mamã. To pronounce a word correctly, it is important to note the length of the vowel sound. For example, mama means "a ring," mamã means "chew it," and mãmã means "light." The word mãmã is pronounced twice as long as mama.

Consonants with peculiar pronunciations are:

b as "mb" in "member"
c as "th" in "father"
d as "nd" in "hand"
g as "ng" in "singer"
j as a slurred "ch"
q as "ng" in "finger"

The consonants k, p, and t are pronounced the same as in English, although they are much softer, and r is always rolled. The letter v is pronounced with the lower lip against the upper lip, somewhere between a v and a b.

Fijians always stress the next to last syllable. Some long words with four or five syllables also take a secondary stress. Not as apparent as the penultimate stress, the secondary stress usually falls on the first or second syllable.

ENGLISH

A major legacy of the British colonial rule is English, one of the official languages of Fiji. Although used mainly in written form rather than spoken, it is understood by almost everybody. All schools teach in English after the third grade. In a country with two main racial groups, English is a nonthreatening and acceptable third language for all official matters. Fijians and Indians usually communicate with each other in English. Most forms of mass media use English, since they reach out to both communities.

A Fijian schoolboy learning to write in English. The standard Fijian alphabet uses all the English letters except "x."

Although Fiji Islanders learn British English at school, the way they speak English is influenced by the language they use at home. The Fijian accent is melodious and rather singsong. After more than 100 years, the English language in Fiji has evolved only slightly, with some words or phrases taking on different meanings. For example, the word "step" means to cut classes. When a Fijian says, "Good luck to you," it does not bear the good wishes usually associated with the phrase. Instead, it means, "Serves you right!"

Since Fiji is composed of many far-flung islands, radio reception is quite patchy, or even nonexistent, in many parts of the archipelago.

NEWSPAPERS

In the wake of the 2006 military coup, press freedom has been severely curtailed and journalists have complained of human rights abuses committed against them by the authorities. The military government has stationed censors in newsrooms to make sure that no story that is critical of the takeover is published.

Although freedom of expression is guaranteed in the Fijian constitution, press freedom has different meanings for the government and the media. The conservative faction of the population and the government itself fear that Western-style media opinions would unsettle the Fijian cultural heritage and harmony. At the same time, the government wants to use modern forms of communication to disseminate information and to promote development.

The main newspaper in Fiji is the English-language *Fiji Times*. Founded in 1869, it now belongs to the influential Australian-owned Murdoch Group. The government-owned *Daily Post*, also in English, focuses on local news. The government also publishes the *Nai Volasiga* in Fijian. Another Fijian paper, the weekly *Nai Lalakai*, is published by *The Fiji Times*. The only Hindi newspaper is a weekly, *Shanti Dut*, also published by *The Fiji Times*.

A man catches up on the daily news with the main newspaper in Fiji, *The Fiji Times*.

RADIO AND TELEVISION

Fiji has two national radio networks. The government-sponsored Fiji Broadcasting Commission runs six radio stations—two each in Fijian, Fiji-Hindi, and English. Of the two English stations, one focuses on news and community issues while the other features music and chat. Bula FM specializes in Fijian music. Recordings of local singers are frequently aired by this station. News broadcasts, however, on all six government-sponsored stations are prepared by employees of the Ministry of Information.

Fijian men enthusiastically cheering a rugby match on television.

The independent provider Communications Fiji Limited broadcasts over five stations, one in Fijian, two in Fiji-Hindi, and two in English. The latter are highly popular as they play English music interspersed with gossip. All five stations are mainly musical in content. In addition, Fijians can also tune in to several foreign stations, such as the BBC, Radio France, or Australia's ABC, as well as regional broadcasters playing Pacific islands music.

Television came to Fiji only in 1991, when Television New Zealand provided a live telecast of World Cup rugby matches. The only broadcaster is Fiji Television. Initially owned by the Fijian government and Television New Zealand, it is now a publicly listed company. Offering very little local content, the sole television station, Fiji One, airs mainly American sitcoms or other English-language shows sourced from the UK and New Zealand. Fiji One is on from midafternoon to early next morning. A clause in their license forbids the station from broadcasting "anything offensive to their Great Council of Chiefs." Only the islands close to Viti Levu can receive television at all.

Fiji TV also owns Sky Pacific, which offers 12 channels, two of which are Indian, showing Bollywood movies, and a single Chinese one. News channels such as CNN and BBC are also available. Since 2007 the Bainimarama government has granted two more television licenses, but the hotly awaited second channel is yet to materialize.

As with the print journalism, Fiji's radio and television are closely monitored by the authorities, and any reportage critical of the government is swiftly punished.

ARTS

Local folk art for sale in Fiji.

FIJIANS ARE A VERY ARTISTIC PEOPLE.

FIJIANS ARE A VERY ARTISTIC PEOPLE. Many villages have kept alive their traditional arts, although for some, the main purpose is to attract tourist money. While traditional arts such as pottery and wood sculpture are still very widely practiced in the country, Fijians have also adopted new and more modern forms of artistic expression.

Young artists are trying their hands at painting and experimenting with different styles. Fashion designing is another new art form, combining Fijian motifs and styles with modern technology. A popular motif used freely by contemporary fashion designers is the hibiscus, the national flower. Other artists have turned to photography, modern dance, and jazz.

A Fijian woman stenciling traditional designs to *masi* cloth.

Opened in 2009, the Fiji Center for the Arts in Suva provides a hub for collaboration with local and international artists. It is a focal point for dance, theater, music, fine art, crafts, and fashion, and the marketing of the arts, bringing together many diverse elements of Fiji's arts and crafts.

POTTERY

Fijian pottery is unique because most of the peoples in the South Pacific region have forgotten how to make pots. Pottery making has been passed down by Fijian women for countless centuries, and different regions have different techniques and styles. Today's center of Fijian pottery is the Sigatoka Valley on Viti Levu.

The pottery methods Fijians use are known as coiling and paddling. The potter cuts out a flat round piece of clay for the bottom of the pot. Using slabs of clay or coils and strips, she builds up the sides. Then she gently knocks the pot into shape with a wooden paddle. A smooth rounded stone inside the pot prevents the sides from caving in. The potter uses paddles of different sizes for different types of pots and for different areas of a single pot. When the potter is satisfied with the shape of the pot, she leaves it to dry indoors for a few days. When dry, the pot is taken outdoors and fired for an hour in an open pit. To seal the pots, a type of resin is applied on the outside surface when it is still hot. While enhancing its watertight capacity, the resin also gives a reddish sheen that brings out the color of the clay.

Pottery making in Fiji was mainly the work of women from seafaring villages, who traded their pots for food and other land products.

LAPITA POTTERY

Lapita pottery is named after an archaeological site of its early discovery in New Caledonia, and is associated with the people who first discovered and settled Fiji. Recovered from archaeological digs throughout the Pacific Ocean, Lapita pottery gives us an idea of the length of time of human settlement in specific areas, as well as how the populations of the different islands are related to one another.

Lapita is an ornate style of pottery used mainly for ceremonial purposes. As Lapita pottery is very fragile, a large number of potsherds have been found in many ancient village sites. The first discoveries were made in New Caledonia in the 1960s. Sherds in this style have been unearthed on islands located in a wide arc of the southwestern Pacific, stretching from Aitape on the Sepik coast of New Guinea all the way eastward to Fiji, Tonga, and Samoa.

The sherds are identified by intricate geometric patterns impressed into the clay prior to firing. Some artifacts display patterns made of dotlike incisions, much like those used in tattooing. The finest example is a clay head recovered in New Ireland, east of Papua New Guinea. The pattern was made by a needle-fine, comblike tool similar to those used by Polynesians in traditional tattooing. Lapita pottery has affinities with Asian pottery, evident in the shape of the jars, but the ornamental design is a local development.

One of the best known Lapita sites in Fiji is in the Sigatoka area, where sand dunes continue to unveil not only artifacts but also human bones. The most ancient potsherds found in Fiji date as far back as 1000 B.C. Other impressive pots have been found on Yanuca Island, at Natunuku, Naigani, and Lakeba.

Lapita pots point to a sophisticated society. By about 500 B.C. Fijian pottery characteristics changed to a simpler form. Patterns were no longer elaborate, as functionality and simplicity came to be valued greater than mere aestheticism. This switch coincided with a shift in population and occupations. Agriculture had increased significantly, as the population continued to grow and expand into interior areas of the islands. Around the same time, intergroup warfare and cannibalism appears to have increased and fortified villages became common. Potters turned to a straightforward variety of decorations that lasted from 100 B.C. to A.D. 1000. Pottery making continued throughout Fiji until the period of European contact. Today pottery is made in only a few villages.

WOODCARVING

Although most Fijians now use factory-made utensils and earthenware, the traditional *tanoa*, which is used for the daily drinking of kava in Fijian households, is still carved out of wood. Nowadays the tourist industry almost alone keeps Fijian woodcarving crafts alive. Many items are carved for sale as souvenirs, including those that are no longer used by the Fijian people, such as cannibal forks or war spears, and even artifacts that were never part of Fijian culture, such as Polynesian tikis (images) and masks.

The people of the Lau Group are the best woodcarvers in Fiji. Items for religious uses are carved out of ironwood, which is considered sacred. Hibiscus wood is much lighter and more easily broken. In the old days, it took years to carve a war club, as the carving was done in the living tree and left to grow into a desired shape. Today steel tools are used. Shells are sometimes rubbed over carvings to give a fine polish on the most exquisite pieces. In areas where the Polynesian influence is strong, carved objects are inlaid with shell, ivory, or bone.

There are many different types of woodcarving. For example, human and animal forms are generally used for such religious objects as *yaqona* vessels.

A wood-carver adds a finishing polish to his work by rubbing shells on the surface.

LITERATURE

Fijians have a very long tradition of storytelling. Myths and legends are passed down from one generation to another in informal storytelling gatherings or around a shared bowl of kava. These stories recount the origins of the Fijian people or explain the nature of plants and animals. One legend is that the coconut has three "eyes" or indentations at the bottom in order to watch out for people below the tree so that it does not drop on them. Traditional stories live in an oral tradition. Apart from some English translations, they have not been written down into books for Fijian children to read or learn. Fortunately, many Fijians still live in traditional villages, so this folklore is not yet in danger of being lost.

Fijian literature is mostly written in English. Although the local literary community is rather small, it is made up of many talented and committed poets, playwrights, and writers. One of the foremost contemporary writers is Joseph Veramu, whose short story collection *The Black Messiah* has been well received in literary circles. His novel *Moving Through the Streets* offers a keen insight into the life of teenagers in Suva. Leading playwrights are Jo Nacola and Rotuma-born Vilsoni Hereniko.

Indian writers express themselves in both Hindi and English. A central thread lacing through all their works is the theme of injustice and the plight of indentured laborers. Prominent Indian writers are Subramani; Satendra Nandan; Raymond Pillai; and Prem Banfal, who writes from the perspective of a woman.

A much-admired traditional story-teller on his way to a festival.

SINGING

Dravuni people singing in a group.

Fijians are amply endowed musically, and they do love to sing! Songs pull together a large part of the people's oral tradition. In the villages local legends are retold through songs. When the missionaries came to Fiji, they introduced hymns and choral singing, which the natives readily embraced. Singing is a traditional island activity, and the villagers felt a close affinity for Christian lyrics and music. Even the smallest village church boasts a choir, and Sunday service singing is fervent and of exceptional quality. Church music includes choices from both Western and traditional repertories, and hymns are sung in English and Fijian. In fact, many new lyrics have been written to traditional music. Although the title of Fiji's national anthem, "God Bless Fiji," resembles the British "God Save the Queen," the song took its music from an old Fijian melody. Nearly all traditional instruments have disappeared, and the most popular musical instrument today is the guitar.

Contemporary singers have also been influenced by modern trends, such as reggae and jazz. Popular performers appear in the major hotels and in nightclubs in Suva. Many of them have also recorded their music on CDs, which are sold in music stores.

As for the Indian community, they are more attracted to songs in Hindi from "Bollywood," the Indian movie industry based in the west Indian megalopolis of Mumbai (Bombay). They like to listen to original recordings of movie music, usually a mixture of Western pop and Indian styles played with traditional and modern instruments. Local Indian singers have also started doing cover versions, or revivals, of popular songs. Indian bands perform Hindi songs at weddings and parties. Classical Indian music is less popular, although the cultural centers offer courses for the tabla, an Indian drum played in pairs, and sitar, a long-necked stringed instrument with a plaintive echoing sound, recognized the world around as "Indian."

Contemporary Fijian music is heavily influenced by Christian hymns, and more and more pop rhythms are finding their way into traditional performances.

MEKE

Meke (MAY-keh) is a traditional performance combining song, dance, and theater. Reenacting legends and stories from Fijian history, mekes were arranged for entertainment and also to welcome visitors or to mark important occasions. Traditional mekes were handed down from one generation to the next, and new ones were composed for specific occasions. Before the missionaries arrived, mekes involved some manner of spiritual domination, with the possessed participants dancing and chanting in a trance.

Men, women, and children take part in a meke, although the sexes perform different dances. When they dance together as in the tralala (trah-LAH-lah), which is a two-step shuffle, men and women dance side by side. Another dance with both sexes participating is the vakamalolo (vah-KUH-mah-LOH-loh), which is performed seated on the floor. Men usually perform war dances. Dressed in grass skirts and with their faces painted black by charcoal, the warriors form a line while brandishing clubs and spears. In the areas where Tongan influence is strong, paddles are also used as accessories. The women's dance is called seasea (SEE-see). Dressed in conservative sulus and blouses, or mission dresses, they sing and dance gracefully with fans. All dancers wear flower necklaces, or leis, and women also adorn themselves with flowers in their hair.

In a Fijian meke, the seating arrangement is very important, just as every movement and gesture during the performance has a special significance. Even the spectators are expected to follow certain rules. Important guests are given special seating positions in order to avoid offense.

ARCHITECTURE

The traditional Fijian house is the *bure*. Usually rectangular in shape, it is made of tightly woven bamboo walls with a thatched roof. In the past, tree fern trunks were used. In eastern Fiji, where Tongan and Samoan influence is strong, circular *bures* can also be found.

Bures are one-room dwellings with few windows and a low door. It is quite dark inside. The packed-earth floor is covered with pandanus mats, and a curtain at one end separates the sleeping area from the living room. Cooking is done in a separate, smaller *bure*. Except for numerous floor mats and some storage containers, the *bure* is bare of furniture, because its occupants sit and sleep on the floor.

Bure building is a traditional skill passed down from father to son. The dwelling is cheap and relatively fast and easy to build. When a family needs a new *bure*, the whole village takes a hand in its construction. Since the house is made of plant materials, the walls and roofs require regular maintenance. This does not mean, though, that the *bure* is a house that can be destroyed easily. It is usually sturdy enough to withstand hurricanes, common occurrences in the islands of Fiji.

Villagers building a *bure*. All the community pitches in to get it made.

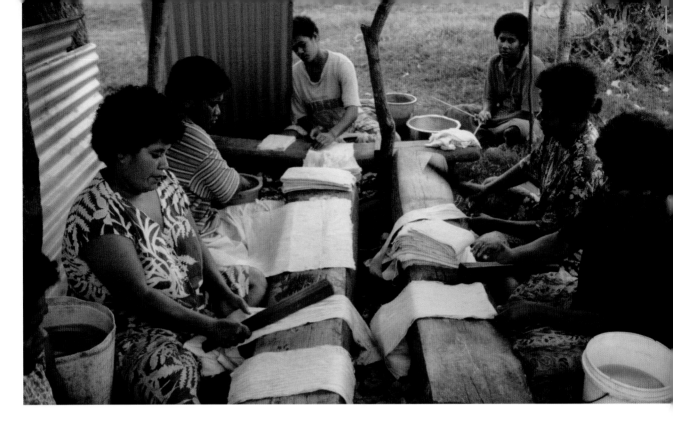

ARTS AND CRAFTS

Weaving is a craft that most village girls learn when young. In some tribes only women can weave. The most common objects are mats, but baskets and hats are also made. Woven items make popular wedding or baptismal presents and are also given to chiefs as a form of tribute. The usual weaving material is pandanus leaf, but coconut husks, banana stems, vine tendrils, and waterweeds are also used. The traditional method for blackening the leaves for contrasting color patterns was to bury them in mud for several days and then boil them with certain other leaves. Today most weavers use chemical dyes.

Another traditional craft that is almost exclusively the domain of women is *masi* making. *Masi* (MAH-sih), also called tapa in Polynesia, is the traditional pounded bark cloth used in Fijian rituals. *Masi* feels like felt. When the cloth is ready, geometric patterns are applied with stencils made from green pandanus and banana leaves. Traditional dyes are rust, obtained from red clay, and black, made from an infusion of candlenut and mangrove bark. Plain *masi* is beige.

Fijian women making *masi*, a beautiful pounded-bark cloth.

LEISURE

Young children showing off in a river near Lovoni.

FIJI ISLANDERS, ESPECIALLY THE indigenous Fijians, live at a relaxed pace, and laid-back activities form an integral part of their lifestyle. Almost no one is caught up in the frenzied race for material well-being.

Most people prefer to enjoy their time in a casual manner, so long as they have the wherewithal to feed, clothe, and shelter their families. Because most leisure activities are simple and inexpensive, or even free, the Fijians do not have to work very hard to be able to afford the little cash needed for a good time.

One of the world's top professional golfers is Vijay Singh, who started out as a caddy for his father. The elder Singh was the club president of the Nadi Airport Golf Club, where his son won his first trophy in 1981.

Friends hanging out together at Sukuna Park in Suva. For many Fijian women, leisure means stopping for a chat with their friends at the market or at the food centers.

Local children enjoying a race in Yaroi.

In Fiji, Western forms of leisure blend with traditional, communal activities. Most men spend their free time practicing or watching a Western sport, but their most popular pastime is drinking kava with a circle of friends. As for the women, spare time revolves around church and other communal activities. Gossiping while working on a group project is probably the most engaging pastime.

SPORTS

Fijians are very enthusiastic about sports, and they play all kinds of Western sports. Sports are banned on Sundays, which are reserved for going to church. Golf is a diversion that has received a lot of international investment, with world-class facilities in some resorts. These posh operations attract mainly wealthy tourists to the islands. Not many Fijians are inclined to take up the game. Former prime minister Sitiveni Rabuka is an avid golfer, though, and it has been rumored that many political moves, including the 1987 coups, were plotted on the golf links.

Another sport that locals and tourists alike love is scuba diving. With its astonishing wealth of coral reefs, Fiji is an important center for diving in the Pacific. Surfing has existed in Fiji for hundreds of years and is another popular activity with both locals and visitors. Windsurfing is also catching on and can be practiced now at more locations than surfing.

Rugby is the prime national pastime, and Fijians take great pride in the national team's achievements. A game similar to American football, it is played by teams of 7, 10, or 15 players. The aim is to score points by touching the ball down between the opponent's goalposts. Rugby players need to be strong and hardy since it is a sport with lots of physical contact. In Fiji rugby is played by Fijians only. The season lasts from April to September.

There is a rugby field in every village, and a game is played almost every week. Visitors are often invited to a friendly match.

Divers are always awestruck by the beauty, vastness, and quiet serenity of the marine life in Fiji.

Rugby is Fiji's national sport and the Fiji Sevens team has won the Rugby World Cup Sevens twice, in 1997 and 2005. When Fiji won the World Cup for the first time, the whole country rejoiced with a public holiday and the government generously financed national celebrations. The Fiji Sevens team has also been the victor of the Hong Kong Sevens Tournament—considered to be the world's premier sevens tournament—10 times since the competition started in 1976. With its win over South Africa in June 2009, Fiji established itself as the most successful team ever in the annual Hong Kong tournament.

In 2009 Fiji won its third consecutive gold in rugby sevens at the World Games, an international multisport competition organized for sports that are not contested in the Olympic Games.

The national rugby team, the 15s, is one of the strongest in the world. Although it has never won the Rugby World Cup, it has qualified for the final rounds several times.

As foreign clubs have the wherewithal to pay much higher salaries than can be offered in Fiji, most of the national players ply their skills elsewhere in the world, mainly in New Zealand and Australia.

There is a difference in the games played in towns and in the countryside. Villagers prefer team games, and volleyball is very popular. Rural Indians like to play cricket. Lawn bowling, a sedate game that suits the Fijian easygoing attitude, is played by older people. Townsfolk like tennis and hockey. Soccer is enjoyed by everyone. Played by Fijians and Indians everywhere in the country, it commands a large following during the playing season, which runs from February to November.

Tourists join local Fijians in a friendly game of beach volleyball.

DRINKING

Drinking kava is hands down the most popular leisure pursuit of Fiji Islanders. Both native Fijians and Indians are devoted to this pastime. Kava is not sold in bottles, as the drink has to be consumed as soon as it is prepared. Its elaborate preparation and the ritual surrounding drinking it is a way of buoying community spirit. Sharing a bowl of kava, with the soft strumming of guitars in the background, participants immediately feel relaxed and close, and a bond naturally forms among them. Drinking kava is the Fijian's link with his ancestral past, the ceremony and devotional ritual having originated in ancient Fijian society. Today, Fijians regard it more as a social activity than a religious rite, though its cultural value is very great.

Fijian men performing the kava ceremony before enjoying the drink together.

In the villages, men and women do not drink kava together. The custom is for men to gather around a large bowl of the mix in a *bure* and talk while drinking. The women do the same, but they confine themselves to the kitchen. Some old women are allowed to join the men in their drinking sessions.

Kava is not an intoxicating liquor, so it does not make the drinkers drunk, and drinking sessions do not degenerate into drunken brawls. The brew is mildly narcotic, however, and the drinker usually feels reluctant to do any kind of work afterward. Its effects range from light-headedness to a mild rush of euphoria. For this reason, government authorities view kava drinking as a social depravity, though it is a custom they still partake in.

Although kava is consumed primarily as a social drink, local healers have used it to treat various ailments, such as tooth decay and respiratory diseases. Kava is also a diuretic, and pharmaceutical manufacturers use it in their formulas. Excessive drinking of kava causes numerous disorders, including loss of appetite, bloodshot eyes, lethargy, restlessness, stomach pains, and scaling of the skin. The latter condition is fairly common among heavy kava drinkers, who may consume up to 10 quarts (9.5 liters) or more daily!

A favorite fund-raising activity in villages is the drinking party. Organizers prepare a certain amount of drink, usually kava, and participants take turns buying drinks for themselves and the other partygoers. To show their sincerity, they spend every single cent in their pockets. Those who cannot handle another round of the brew can get out of drinking it by offering a reward for someone else to down the kava. Of course, the extra money goes into the kitty being raised and not to the drinker. Aside from being a merry gathering, the drinking party also brings the community together in an activity that will benefit everybody. School fees for the village children often are raised this way.

Because of the congenial nature of the drinking , many business deals or contacts are made while sharing kava. There is always a bowl of kava in government offices for the staff to dip into during their breaks. Visitors are also offered a *bilo*, or cup. Most employees have their own *bilo*, which they keep at the office. In the old days there used to be a bowl of kava in the back balcony of the parliament building for the legislators to share. Many police stations hold nightly kava drinking sessions when things are quiet. There are also stories of magistrates imbibing their favorite drink while hearing court cases.

Although beer and other types of liquor are available in Fiji, kava is the popular choice at social gatherings, parties, and religious ceremonies. Cultivation of the kava plant is a prosperous enterprise for farmers all over the archipelago.

Drinking is also done at private clubs, a relic behavior from colonial days. Although prominent signs proclaim, "Members Only," they are actually open to any well-dressed visitor. The drinks of choice in the clubs are beer and other liquor, not kava.

Fijians believe that drinking and singing go hand in hand. No celebration or gathering is complete without them both.

FESTIVALS

Fijian traditional warrior attire worn during a festival.

ALTHOUGH FIJI IS A RATHER austere society, Fiji Islanders know how to enjoy themselves throughout the year. Religious festivals of the larger Christian, Hindu, and Muslim congregations are each celebrated with a public holiday.

Fijian festivals may not reach the carnival-like heights of those at other islands in the Pacific, but they are highly colorful and allow the communities to let their hair down. Hindu festivals, in particular, give rise to lively public celebration and merrymaking. Secular holidays, such as New Year's Day, are also celebrated with much gaiety throughout the islands.

Although not a true festival, a *meke* celebration at Navotua village is always enjoyed.

Fiji celebrates 12 official holidays a year. These are mainly historical and religious in context. Apart from fixed dates such as New Year's Day or Christmas, the other holidays are observed on a Monday or Friday so that everyone can benefit from a long weekend. In addition to national holidays, Fijians also take a day off from school or work to celebrate cultural festivals.

New Year's Day—January 1
Prophet Muhammad's Birthday—variable according to Islamic calendar
National Youth Day—end of March
Good Friday—March/April
Easter Saturday—March/ April
Easter Monday—March/ April
Ratu Sir Lala Sukuna Day—end of May
Queen's Birthday—mid-June
Fiji Day—2nd week of October
Diwali—November
Christmas Day—December 25
Boxing Day—December 26

CHRISTMAS

The most important festival in the year for Christians is Christmas. For this pious group, the birth of Christ is the greatest occasion for rejoicing, and most of them attend church on both Christmas Eve and Christmas Day. On Christmas Eve, well-practiced church choirs sing beautiful carols, and the whole congregation joins in. Children, turned out in their best clothes, happily look forward to this day, when they receive presents of toys and books from Santa Claus.

The Fijians' love of food is reflected in all their festive celebrations, thus much feasting takes place during these two days, with kava and traditional

Fijian dishes being the highlights at every table. Villages throw huge communal parties, while people in towns attend smaller gatherings at friends' homes or in hotels. Many parties feature *lovo* (LOH-voh), which is food cooked in a traditional underground pit.

On Christmas Day and Boxing Day, December 25 and 26, many Fijians go to the beach for picnics and parties. Besides an opportunity to unwind, this is also a time to think about the things they have done in the past year and prepare for the challenges ahead. It is also a good time for family and friends to get together. The festive mood continues until New Year's Day, which is celebrated by everyone in Fiji. In some villages the partying lasts for a week or even the whole month of January!

On Rotuma the local version of caroling is the *fara*. Every evening from December 1, bands of children wander from house to house, singing *fara* (traditional) songs and clapping their hands. They are usually rewarded with gifts of perfume, talcum powder, or fruit such as watermelon. But if their singing is poor, the householders throw water on them to chase them away!

A church choir celebrates Christmas by singing traditional carols.

DIWALI

Diwali is the Hindu festival of lights. Literally meaning "a row of lights," Diwali celebrates the triumph of good over evil and light over darkness. Today Diwali is observed on a moonless night in October or November, one of the darkest nights in the year.

Weeks before the festival, Hindu families start to clean their homes and prepare little oil lamps, candles, or special electric lights to decorate their homes. On the morning of Diwali, everyone puts on new clothes and distributes cakes and candies to neighbors and friends. Fruit and candies are also offered to Lakshmi, the goddess of wealth and beauty. Hindus believe that the goddess comes to visit earth on Diwali night following the lighting of the oil lamps and that she will enter only the homes that have been properly cleaned. In the evening everyone gathers at the family shrine to recite prayers and make offerings to Lakshmi. The children's foreheads are daubed with red powder, and the women draw good luck patterns with colored powders outside the front door. As night falls, the lamps are lit, and every Hindu home glitters as in a fairy tale.

An Indian-Fijian dance group during Diwali festivities in November.

OTHER ETHNIC FESTIVALS

Hindus celebrate Holi, the Festival of Colors, in a big way. This festival marks the arrival of spring in India, and is celebrated in February or March in Fiji, at the same time as spring in India. Indian villages are awash with color as everyone has a good time throwing colored water or powders on friends and neighbors. Whole neighborhoods dance in the streets, embrace each other, and exchange playful greetings.

Muslim festivals are much less jubilant, being times to pray and strengthen relationships. Although only the birth of the Prophet Muhammad is a public holiday, Muslims also celebrate Eid al-Fitr and Eid al-Adha. The former marks the end of Ramadan, the fasting month, and the latter commemorates the willingness of Abraham to sacrifice his son to God.

In the Chinese community, Chinese New Year is celebrated with lion dances and much merrymaking. There is plenty of good food, and friends and relatives visit one another, wearing new clothes.

Indian Fijians celebrating Holi at a temple, dusting one another with colored powders.

During Chinese New Year, parents and older folks will give each child a red envelope containing a token sum of money, as a symbol of good luck.

HIBISCUS FESTIVAL

Started in 1956, the Suva Hibiscus Festival was based loosely on Hawaii's Aloha Week. The festival lasts a full week in August and brings together cultural performances by local and foreign groups, a glamorous beauty pageant, and a charity fund-raising drive. Every year the lord mayor of Suva declares the festival open, whereupon a parade kicks off the celebrating, followed at night by a display of fireworks in Albert Park, in central Suva.

Fashion shows, food tasting, music, dancing, and games dominate this festival. The highlight, however, is the Miss Hibiscus pageant. Taking place over two evenings, the aim of the pageant is to find the best ambassador for the city of Suva. Contestants are judged not just on their physical attributes but also on their knowledge of current affairs and their familiarity with Suva. The judges question the contestants on various topics to assess their command of information. A Miss Charity is also crowned to honor the contestant who has raised the greatest amount of money for the Hibiscus Charity Chest. The proceeds collected from the charity drive are distributed to the needy in Fiji.

A daylong children's carnival caters to the youngsters. Babies are entered in a baby show, and prizes are awarded to the most adorable tots and their parents. Older children take part in an aerobics championship contest, and some of them participate in musical and dance performances and fashion shows. It is a fun-filled and lively carnival that many children happily await.

Since Fiji is largely a Christian country, no event is complete without a religious component. The Hibiscus Festival features singing competitions between very accomplished church choirs, and religious worship led by youth organizations and church groups. These exciting presentations usually draw many entrants.

The Hibiscus Festival is a much-loved occasion. Here the Fijians (above) and the Polynesian dancers (opposite) are enjoying themselves tremendously with song and dance.

VULA I BALOLO

Although not a festival in the strictest sense, Vula i Balolo, or the rising of the *balolo*, is a yearly event that villagers in the outer islands and coastal areas eagerly look forward to. *Balolo* is the Fijian name given to *Eunice viridis*, also known as the palolo worm, which lives deep in the coral reef. Measuring about 12 inches (30 cm) in length, this sea worm looks like spaghetti underwater.

Two nights a year, once in October and again in November, millions of *balolo* burrowed in the coral reef release their tails, which rise to the surface of the ocean to mate, turning the sea into a writhing mass of red, green, and brown. The villagers, who had been lying in wait in their boats, immediately pounce on the tails, scooping them up into buckets, wicker baskets, or plastic containers. To the Fijians, the *balolo* tails, full of either sperm or eggs, are rare delicacies, the taste of which recalls that of caviar. It can be eaten raw or fried. The villagers need to work fast for the worm tails melt into a gooey mass with the first rays of the sun and sink back down to the bottom.

The traditional Fijian calendar can pinpoint the rising dates of the *balolo* with unerring accuracy. The first rising occurs in early October when only a few of these creatures appear and the Fijians refer to it as Little Balolo. The next showtime, Big Balolo, happens at the high tide of the full moon, usually between November 20 and 25, and this is when whole villages pour out to feast. Throughout Fiji's recorded history, the *balolo* have never failed to rise on these two appointed nights.

When the *balolo* come up, shoals of fish converge onto the reefs, vying with the local villagers for their share of the delicacy. On Vanua Levu, Vula i Balolo coincides with the arrival of a small deep-sea fish called *deu*, which swim up the mangrove estuaries to lay their eggs. Women in the villages along the southeast coast gather in the rivers to catch the tasty fish.

FOOD

A young boy selling fruit and vegetables at Suva Municipal Market.

CHAPTER 13

F

IJIAN FOOD BRINGS together all the various influences from the country's diversified population. Fijian, Indian, Polynesian, Chinese, and Western cuisines can all be found in the country.

In the villages, the predominant ethnic groups usually keep to their traditional diets, but urban Fijians get to sample different types of foods. Suva and Nadi have all kinds of restaurants, catering to every taste and budget. Even American-style fast food has found its way to Fiji. No truly Fijian dish has evolved from the fraternity of so many culinary traditions. Only Chinese curries combine two separate cuisines—Chinese and Indian.

In general, only native Fijians and Indians eat with their hands. The other communities use spoons and forks. Very few people eat British style, with both a knife and fork used simultaneously. In the villages, meals are eaten on the floor, with the family sitting on mats. When entertaining, Fiji Islanders believe that they should provide enough for their guests to eat their fill—the result is usually too much food. Some hosts even wait for their guests to finish eating before starting on their own meals.

Dried grains and other products are daily staples and essential ingredients in many Fijian meals.

Fijians, Chinese, and Europeans do not have any dietary restrictions, eating the meats and vegetables available in the markets. The Indian community, however, deals with restrictions on what they are free to eat. Muslims do not eat pork and are not supposed to drink alcoholic beverages. Some young Muslim men, however, partake of kava and beer. As for Hindus, tradition encourages them to avoid eating beef, but this restriction is observed only in the most conservative families. Some Hindus are vegetarians.

A villager preparing a *lovo*, the traditional Fijian earth oven, in the village of Navivi, for a community feast also called a *lovo*.

THE FIJIAN OVEN

The Fijian equivalent of the Hawaiian luau is called *lovo*. The whole village works together to prepare this feast. First a large pit is dug and lined with a deep layer of dry coconut husks. The husks are set on fire, and once the fire is going well, stones are heaped on top. When most of the husks have burned away and the stones are very hot, the food, wrapped in banana leaves, is lowered into the pit. Fish and meat are the first to go in, then the vegetables are placed on top. Everything is covered with banana leaves and more hot stones, and the food is left to cook. After about two and a half hours, when everything is cooked, the top leaves and stones are removed.

A popular dish cooked in the *lovo is palusami* (pah-loo-SAH-mih). A mixture of chicken or corned beef with onions, tomatoes, and coconut cream, the *palusami* is wrapped in taro leaves before cooking. At times a whole pig is cooked in the pit. The animal is cleaned and stuffed with banana leaves and hot stones. This method cooks the meat inside and out.

Lovos are still prepared in the villages for special occasions, such as the inauguration of a new chief or a wedding or for such grand festivals as Christmas Day. They are now more often organized in resort hotels, however, accompanied by a *meke* or a fire-walking ceremony.

STAPLES

The universal staple food in Fiji is rice, which is eaten by all the different ethnic groups. The country aims to be self-sufficient in rice by turning over large areas of sugarcane fields to rice cultivation, but more than a third of the total demand is still imported. Indians also eat roti, a flat tortilla-like unleavened bread made of wheat flour and cooked on a griddle. As for the Fijians, a number of starchy roots and tubers go into their diet. Yams are considered a prestigious food, although they are not as nutritious as taro or breadfruit. Taro is usually boiled, but breadfruit, which is an important food that's found everywhere in the South Pacific, can also be baked or roasted. When cooked, breadfruit tastes like bread. Fijians also like to eat boiled yam, sweet potatoes, and cassava. *Vakalolo* (vah-kah-LOH-loh) is a sweet pudding made with all the starchy roots that Fijians eat. Mashed taro, cassava, and breadfruit are combined with coconut milk and caramelized sugarcane juice to make this special delicacy, which is usually served only at traditional feasts.

Many Indian desserts contain coconut. Coconut is used in both Fijian and Indian cooking.

For protein, Fijians consume large amounts of lagoon fish that the families catch themselves. Fish is eaten raw in a salad or baked in coconut cream with taro and cassava. Beef and pork are occasionally fried and eaten with these roots. Chicken, called "bird meat," is not very popular among Fijians. Exotic meats that are still consumed in Fiji include turtle and bat. Although turtles are an endangered species and are protected by law, turtle meat can still be found in the markets. Boiled bat, a foul-smelling and vile-tasting dish, used to be very popular in Fiji. Today, however, only the older generation tolerates it.

Hindus prefer lamb or goat meat cooked in spicy curries. Muslims, on the other hand, cook their curries with beef. Indians also consume large amounts of yellow or red lentils. Cooked in soups and flavored with spices, lentils account for a good portion of their protein intake.

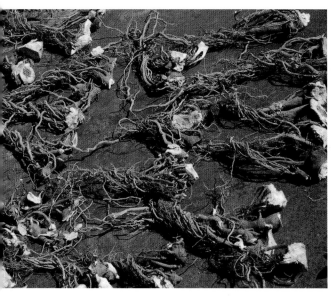

Pepper plant roots drying in the sun will be ground up to make kava. The Fijian lifestyle calls for excessive use of kava.

Both Fijians and Indians have garden vegetables in their diets. Cabbage, beans, and eggplant are either stewed or cooked in curry. Fijians like taro leaves cooked in coconut cream.

Coconut is a very popular plant in Fiji. Its water is drunk as a refreshing beverage, while the grated meat is soaked in boiling water and then squeezed to produce cream or milk. An ecologically destructive dish is millionaire's salad, made from the heart of the coconut tree. To make one salad, a whole mature tree is felled.

The Fijian diet includes increasingly large amounts of canned foods. In many communities, the switch from fresh fruit and vegetables to the canned varieties is a growing cause for concern. Canned beef or sardines have been substituted for fresh meat in many traditional recipes. This reliance on canned foods with excessive fat and salt is giving rise to many diseases that were not present in Fiji a few decades ago.

DRINKS

Although very slightly narcotic, kava is an integral part of Fiji's culture. It must be drunk indoors, as drinking alcoholic beverages on the street is prohibited. Strict laws govern the sale of beer and liquor—for instance, alcohol cannot be sold on Sundays. The most popular drink, after kava, is Fiji Bitter beer, brewed in Suva and Lautoka. Local distilleries produce gin, brandy, rum, vodka, and whisky.

The national drink of choice is kava. Made by diluting the pounded root of the pepper plant in water, it looks and tastes like muddy water. Fijians swear that hand-pounded kava tastes better than the machine-ground root. Most of what is available on the market, though, is turned out by machine and sold in small packets for instant mixing with a bowl of water.

There is a wide choice of nonalcoholic beverages. Coconut water is a favorite, while manufactured soda in every flavor is consumed in large quantities. Although fresh fruit is readily available, freshly squeezed fruit juice is not popular. Fijians prefer to drink fruit cordial diluted with water.

MARKETS

Fijians buy their produce from a variety of sources. They can get a few vegetables from an Indian housewife selling garden produce in her front yard or visit the market or supermarket. All the towns have a municipal market as well as a well-stocked supermarket. Villagers are usually self-sufficient in fresh produce.

The Suva Municipal Market is the largest retail produce market in the Pacific. Polynesian, Chinese, Indian, and Fijian vendors sell fish, meat, vegetables, fruit, coconut oil, and nearly everything else that a Fijian household might need. The ground floor contains all the fresh meats and vegetables, while dried goods are found upstairs. Large areas are devoted to the sale of kava, whole and ground. The Indian spices section is a heady mix of aromas and colors. Indian sweets are sold from kiosks at one side of the market. Some of the confections are actually not sweet but spicy. There is also a *yaqona* saloon dedicated solely to kava drinkers. Passersby are urged to try a bowl by energetic salesmen. Fijian women also sell fresh pineapple and guava juice from glass containers.

A two-story structure, the renowned Suva Municipal Market also sells colorful handicrafts. It is one of the few places where all races in the country are represented.

The Lautoka town market in Viti Levu, selling great piles of fresh produce.

PALUSAMI (CORNED BEEF IN TARO LEAVES)

4 servings

1 can (12 ounces/375 ml) of corned beef

1 cup (250 ml) finely chopped onions

2 tablespoons (30 ml) butter

1 can (8 ounces/250 ml) of unsweetened
   coconut milk

2 medium tomatoes, diced

10 young taro leaves or 2 pounds
   of fresh spinach

Aluminium foil

- Line the bottom of an 8- or 9-inch-square baking pan with half the total amount of taro or spinach leaves.

- Sauté the onions in butter until tender.

- Mix the cooked onions with corned beef, tomatoes, and up to 8 ounces (250 ml) of unsweetened coconut milk.

- Pour the mixture over the leaves, and top with the remaining leaves.

- Cover pan tightly with foil and bake at 350°F (183°C) for 30—45 minutes.

VAKALOLO (FIJIAN PUDDING)

4 servings

4 cups (1L) freshly grated cassava

1 cup (250 ml) freshly grated coconut

¼ inch freshly grated ginger

1 cup (250 ml) sugar

6 cloves (optional)

Aluminium foil

- Mix all five ingredients together.
- Divide mixture into four equal parts. Wrap each pile in foil.
- Place the sealed parcels on a rack over simmering water. Steam the parcels for 40 minutes.
- Unwrap and serve.

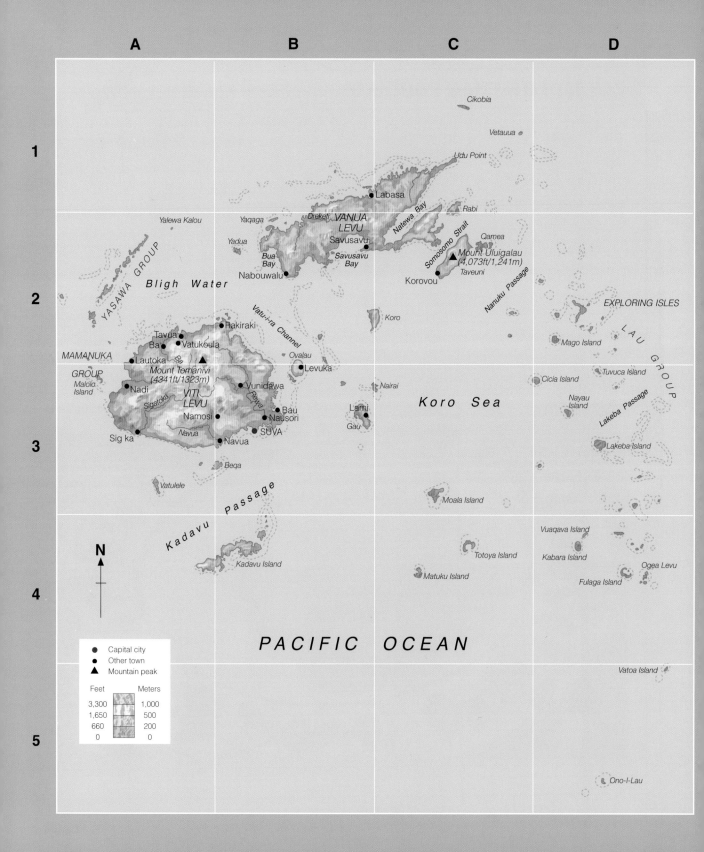

	A	B	C	D

1

Cikobia

Vetauua

Udu Point

Labasa

2

Yalewa Kalou

Yaqaga

Drekeli *VANUA LEVU*

Natewa Bay *Rabi*

Yadua

Savusavu

Qamea

Bua Bay

Savusavu Bay

Somosomo Strait ▲ Mount Uluigalau (4,073ft/1,241m)

Nabouwalu

Taveuni

Korovou

YASAWA GROUP

Bligh Water

Nanuku Passage

EXPLORING ISLES

Koro

LAU GROUP

Rakiraki

Vatu-i-ra Channel

Mago Island

Tavua

Ba Vatukoula

Ovalau

Lautoka

Levuka

Nairai

Cicia Island *Tuvuca Island*

MAMANUKA GROUP

Mount Tomanivi (4341ft/1323m)

▲

Nayau Island

Lakeba Passage

Malolo Island

Nadi

VITI LEVU

Vunidawa

Rewa

Lami *Koro Sea*

Sigatoka

Namosi Bau

Gau

Nausori

SUVA

Lakeba Island

3

Sig ka

Navua

Navua

Beqa

Moala Island

Vatulele

Vuaqava Island

Kadavu *Passage*

Totoya Island

Kabara Island

Ogea Levu

Matuku Island

Fulaga Island

N

↑

Kadavu Island

4

● Capital city
● Other town
▲ Mountain peak

PACIFIC OCEAN

Vatoa Island

Feet		Meters
3,300		1,000
1,650		500
660		200
0		0

5

Ono-I-Lau

MAP OF FIJI

ECONOMIC FIJI

Services	Agriculture	Natural Resources
Airport	Copra	Copper
Hydropower	Ginger	Gold
Ports	Rice	Timber
Tourism	Sugar	Water

ABOUT THE ECONOMY

OVERVIEW

Fiji's economy has been battered by four coups d'etat in 20 years that brought the country to a standstill each time. After each coup, foreign investment shrank to a trickle and tourist arrivals dropped. Most donor countries cut off financial aid, and Fijian goods ran the risk of being boycotted on world markets. As the Fijian economy is highly dependent on a few Western countries (Australia, the United States, and the UK), Japan, and the EU (for sugar), slowdown in these markets affects Fiji quite badly. The Fijian economy today is beset with overreliances on sugar, tourism, and remittances from Fijians working overseas.

GROSS DOMESTIC PRODUCT (GDP)

$3.59 billion (2009 estimate)

GDP PER CAPITA

$3,800 (2009 estimate)

CURRENCY

Fiji dollar
F$1=100 cents ($1=F$1.90, 2009 estimate)

LABOR FORCE

335,000 (2007 estimate)

UNEMPLOYMENT RATE

7.6 percent (1999 estimate)

TOURISM

585,031 visitors (2008 estimate)
Revenue: $462 million (2008 estimate)

GROWTH RATE

0.2 percent (2008 estimate)

INFLATION

6.32 percent (2008 estimate)

NATURAL RESOURCES

Timber, gold, silver, copper, fish, beaches, hydropower, potential offshore oil

AGRICULTURAL PRODUCTS

Sugar, timber, copra, coconut oil, root crops, rice, fruits and vegetables, ginger

MAIN INDUSTRIES

Tourism, sugar, clothing, copra, gold, silver, lumber

MAIN EXPORTS

Sugar, canned fish, bottled water, garments, unrefined gold, coconut oil, copra, timber, and ginger

MAIN IMPORTS

Manufactured goods, fuels, machinery and transportation equipment, electrical appliances and parts, chemicals, and food

MAIN TRADE PARTNERS

Australia, New Zealand, United States, Japan, European Union

CULTURAL FIJI

Momi Gun Battery
Built in 1941 to protect Fiji from a possible Japanese invasion, the battery contains two six-inch guns, one of which is rumored to have been used in the Boer War and the other during World War I.

Navala Village
The last remaining thatched hut village in Fiji decided in 1950 to reject modern building materials. All youth are encouraged to learn the traditional art of *bure* making.

Cession Site
Here King Cakobau signed the Deed of Cession in 1874, handing over the sovereignty of Fiji to Great Britain as well as his iconic war club.

Garden of the Sleeping Giant
Originally designed to house actor Raymond Burr's private collection of tropical orchids, the garden showcases more than 2,000 different varieties of orchids, covering 50 acres (20 ha).

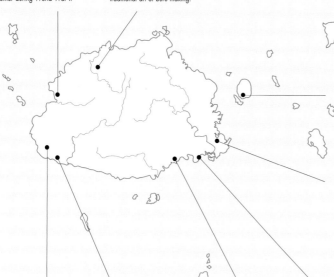

Tavuni Hill Fort
Built by a Tongan chief in the 18th century, this best example of a traditional Fijian fort offers a glimpse into what war was like in olden times. Restored exhibits include cooking ovens, waste pits, and even a killing stone.

Sigatoka Sand Dunes
Stretching over several miles, these dunes were an ancient burial ground. Archaeological findings include Lapita pottery.

Laucala Ring-Ditch Fort
The fort was built in the 18th century to protect the settlement from people migrating from the interior. The site is unique for its double fortification—two ring-ditch forts side by side.

Fiji Museum
The best museum in Fiji displays a double-hulled war canoe in its grand hall. Other exhibits include cannibal forks, war clubs, and tattooing tools. The Indo-Fijian Gallery recounts the history of Indian indentured laborers brought to Fiji.

ABOUT THE CULTURE

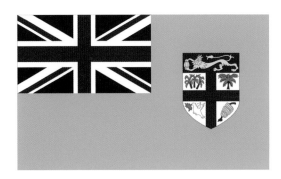

OFFICIAL NAME
Republic of the Fiji Islands

AREA
Total Area: 501,800 square miles (1,300,000 square km); Land Area: 7,056 square miles (18,274 square km)

CAPITAL
Suva

MAJOR CITIES
Suva, Nadi, Lautoka, Nausori, Sigatoka, Levuka, Labasa, Savusavu

PROVINCES
One dependency, Rotuma, and 14 provinces: Ba, Bua, Cakaudrove, Kadavu, Lau, Lomaiviti, Macuata, Nadroga-Navosa, Naitasiri, Namosi, Ra, Rewa, Serua, Tailevu

MAJOR RIVERS
Rewa, Sigatoka, Ba

HIGHEST POINT
Mount Tomanivi (4,341 feet/1,323 m)

POPULATION
944,720 people (2009 estimate)

LIFE EXPECTANCY
Total population: 70.73 years
Male: 68.18 years
Female: 73.41 years (2009 estimate)

BIRTHRATE
21.92 births per 1,000 population (2009 estimate)

DEATH RATE
5.66 deaths per 1,000 population (2009 estimate)

INFANT MORTALITY RATE
11.58 deaths per 1,000 population (2009 estimate)

FERTILITY RATE
2.65 children born per woman (2009 estimate)

ETHNIC GROUPS
Fijian (57.3 percent), Indian (37.6 percent), other Pacific Islanders (3.3 percent), part European (1.0 percent), Chinese (0.5 percent), European (0.3 percent)

MAJOR RELIGIONS
Christian (64.7 percent), Hindu (27.9 percent), Muslim (6.3 percent), Sikh (0.3 percent), others or none (0.8 percent)

MAJOR LANGUAGES
English, Fijian, Hindi

TIME LINE

IN FIJI	IN THE WORLD
1000 B.C.	
Austronesian settlers arrive from the west.	**1206–1368**
A.D. 1300–1800s	Genghis Khan unifies the Mongols and starts
Tongan incursions from the east.	conquest of the world. At its height, the Mongol
Dutch seafarer Abel Tasman sights Vanua Levu.	Empire under Kublai Khan stretches from China
1774	to Persia and parts of Europe and Russia.
Captain James Cook visits Vatoa.	**1776**
1808	U.S. Declaration of Independence
Swedish mercenary Charles Savage arrives at Bau and provides guns to Chief Tanoa in successful wars to conquer western Fiji.	
1822	
European settlement begins at Levuka.	
1830	
First Christian missionaries arrive at Lakeba.	
1848	
Prince Enele Ma'afu wrests control of eastern Fiji from Lau Group.	
1853	
Cakobau installed as high chief of Bau.	
1867	**1861**
Unrest grows; Cakobau installed as king of Bau; Rev. Thomas Baker is eaten by cannibals.	The U.S. Civil War begins.
1868	**1869**
Polynesia Company buys Suva in exchange for paying Cakobau's debts.	The Suez Canal is opened.
1871	
Central government formed at Levuka, makes Cakobau king of Fiji.	
1874	
Cakobau's government collapses; cedes Fiji to Britain without a price tag.	
1875	
Sir Arthur Gordon becomes first governor of Fiji.	
1879	
First Indians arrive as indentured laborers.	
1882	
Capital moved from Levuka to Suva.	**1914**
1916	World War I begins.
Recruitment of indentured labor ends.	
1917–18	
Fijian soldiers support Allies in World War I.	

IN FIJI	IN THE WORLD
1942–45 Fijians excel as jungle scouts with Allied military in World War II.	**1945** The United States drops atomic bombs on Hiroshima and Nagasaki, Japan. World War II ends.
1956 First Legislative Council established, with Ratu Sir Lala Sukuna as speaker.	
1966 Fijian-dominated Alliance Party wins Fiji's first elections.	
1970 Fiji becomes independent; Ratu Sir Kamisese Mara chosen as first prime minister.	**1986** Nuclear power disaster at Chernobyl in Ukraine
1987 Fijian-Indian coalition wins majority in election, with Indian-majority cabinet. Sitiveni Rabuka stages two bloodless military coups. Ratu Sir Penaia Ganilau becomes first president.	**1991** Breakup of the Soviet Union
1992 Rabuka's party wins election, making him prime minister.	**1997** Hong Kong is returned to China.
1999 Mahendra Chaudhry elected Fiji's first Indian prime minister.	
2000 George Speight leads coup and takes the cabinet hostage. Military disbands constitution, appoints interim Fijian-led government headed by Laisenia Qarase.	
2001 Qarase wins majority in new elections.	**2001** Terrorists crash planes in New York, Washington, D.C., and Pennsylvania.
2002 Speight found guilty of treason, sentenced to life imprisonment.	
2002–04 Qarase proposes "reconciliation" bill.	**2003** War in Iraq begins.
2006 Army chief Frank Bainimarama overthrows Qarase and installs Chaudhry as finance minister.	
2007 Bainimarama appointed interim prime minister.	**2008** The first black president of the United States, Barack Obama, is elected.
2009 Bainimarama promises elections for 2014.	
2010 Fiji government in transition.	

GLOSSARY

bilo (MBIH-loh)
A bowl made from half a coconut shell.

bula (MBU-lah)
A common Fijian greeting, meaning "life."

bure (MBOO-reh)
A traditional Fijian thatched dwelling.

choli (CHOH-lih)
A short, tight blouse worn with the sari by Indian women.

dhoti
A white loincloth worn by Indian men.

kava
A slightly sedating drink made from the dried roots of the pepper plant.

kerekere (kay-reh-KAY-ray)
A Fijian folkway of seeking favors from relatives.

lovo (LOH-voh)
A feast cooked by hot stones in a covered underground pit also called *lovo*.

masi (MAH-sih)
A traditional pounded bark cloth with a smooth and feltlike finish.

mataqali (mah-tang-GAH-lee)
An extended family group.

meke (MAY-keh)
A traditional performance combining song, dance, and theater.

roti
A flat tortilla-like bread made of wheat flour and cooked on a griddle.

sari
A traditional garment of Indian women, worn as a full, wraparound skirt with one end draped over the left shoulder.

sulu (SOO-loo)
A wraparound skirt worn by adults, short for men and long for women.

tabla
An Indian drum played in pairs.

tabua (TAM-bwah)
A polished whale tooth used as a diplomatic gift in traditional society.

tanoa (TAH-nwah)
A large wooden bowl for ceremonial mixing of kava.

vakalolo (vah-kah-LOH-loh)
A sweet pudding of cassava, taro, and breadfruit.

yaqona (yang-GOH-nah)
An elaborate ceremony for drinking kava.

FOR FURTHER INFORMATION

BOOKS

Aporosa, S. G. *Yaqona (Kava) and Education in Fiji: A Clash of Cultures?* Saarbrücken, Germany: VDM Verlag, 2008.

Kelly, Keith. *Letters from Fiji: A Peace Corps Memoir*. Nashville, IN: Lotus Petal Publishing, 2009.

Nimmerfroh, Achim. *Fiji's Wild Beauty: A Photographic Guide to Coral Reefs of the South Pacific*. Hackenheim, Germany: Conchbooks, 2006.

Thomson, Peter. *Kava in the Blood: A Personal & Political Memoir from the Heart of Fiji*. North Charleston, SC: BookSurge, 2008.

Troost, J. Maarten. *Getting Stoned with Savages: A Trip Through the Islands of Fiji and Vanuatu*. New York: Broadway Books, 2006.

FILMS

Tom Vendetti. *Fiji Firewalkers*. Vendetti Productions, 2006.

Grant Brown. *Pirate Islands: The Lost Treasure of Fiji*. H.O.M. Vision, 2007.

MUSIC

Various Artists. *Fiji: Independence Day.* Blind Man Sound, 2007.

Various Artists. *Fiji: Indigenous Life*. Indigenous Alliance, 2008.

Various Artists. *Music of the Fiji Islands*. Arc Music, 2005.

Various Artists. *Fiji: Xperience*. Blind Man Sound, 2007.

BIBLIOGRAPHY

BOOKS

Brenner, Richard and Carrie Miller. *Fiji* (Fodor's In Focus). NY: Random House, 2008.

Geraghty, Paul. *Fijian* (Lonely Planet Phrasebook). Melbourne: Lonely Planet, 2008.

Kelly, John D. and Martha Kaplan. *Represented Communities: Fiji and World Decolonization*. Chicago: University Of Chicago Press, 2001.

Mahaney, Casey and Astrid Witte Mahaney. Fiji (Lonely Planet Diving and Snorkeling). Melbourne: Lonely Planet, 2000.

Nicole, Robert. *Disturbing History: Resistance in Early Colonial Fiji, 1874-1914.* Honolulu: University of Hawaii Press, 2009.

Osborn, Ian. *The Rough Guide to Fiji.* London: Rough Guides, 2008.

Ryan, Paddy. *Fiji's Natural Heritage.* Wollombi, New South Wales: Exisle Publishing, 2000.

Stanley, David. *Fiji* (Moon Handbooks). Berkeley, CA: Avalon Travel Publishing, 2007.

Starnes, Dean and Nana Luckham. *Fiji* (Lonely Planet Country Guide). Melbourne: Lonely Planet, 2009.

Trnka, Susanna. *State of Suffering: Political Violence and Community Survival in Fiji.* Ithaca, NY: Cornell University Press, 2008.

WEBSITES

Airports Fiji. www.airportsfiji.com

BBC News: Fiji. http://news.bbc.co.uk/2/hi/americas/country_profiles/1300477.stm

BulaMe. www.bulafiji.com

CIA World Factbook. www.cia.gov/cia/publications/factbook/index.html

Fiji Government Online Portal. www.fiji.gov.fj

Fiji Green. www.fijigreen.com

Fiji Guide. www.fijiguide.com

Fiji Islands Bureau of Statistics. www.statsfiji.gov.fj

Fiji Meteorological Service. www.met.gov.fj\

Fiji Times Online. www.fijitimes.com

Fiji Village. www.fijivillage.com

National Trust of Fiji Islands. www.nationaltrust.org.fj

Parliament of Fiji Islands. www.parliament.gov.fj/main/index.aspx

Reserve Bank of Fiji. www.reservebank.gov.fj

U.S. Department of State. www.state.gov/r/pa/ei/bgn/1834.htm

U.S. Department of State, Travel State. http://travel.state.gov/travel/cis_pa_tw/cis/cis_1114.html

World Health Organization: Fiji. www.who.int/countries/fji/en

INDEX

INDEX